AUDIT RISK ASSESSMENT MADE EASY

© 2021 Charles Hall. All rights reserved. No portion of this book may be reproduced, stored in a retrieval system, or transmitted in any form or by any means—electronic, mechanical, photocopy, recording, scanning, or other—without permission of the author.

While every precaution has been taken in the preparation of this book, the author assumes no responsibility for errors or omissions, or for damages resulting from the use of the information contained herein.

ISBN-13: 978-0-578-96167-5
ISBN-10: 9798486385148

PRAISE FOR
Audit Risk Assessment Made Easy

Too often auditors perform risk assessment procedures as a check-the-box compliance exercise, perhaps because genuine risk assessments require an intimidating amount of professional judgment. In Audit Risk Assessment Made Easy, Charles walks us gently through the process using helpful examples and anecdotes. In so doing, he makes a persuasive case that risk assessment is the key to performing audits that are both effective and efficient.

Dr. Eddie Thomas
Georgia College & State University
Milledgeville, Georgia

Charles clearly recognizes that the CPA's world of auditing has its own specific, highly technical language many might call "auditor-ese" that can over complicate and confuse. Audit practitioners need to more easily visualize and more fully comprehend the application of risk assessment into professional and effective action steps. Charles' writing style communicates that even the most complicated task is so much easier to understand and undertake when it is explained and described in simple language with practical examples.

By taking a page from the Mark Twain method to describe fence painting and Mississippi rafting, Charles breaks risk assessment down into understandable, manageable and effective steps, using uncomplicated declarative sentences, plotting a path to help to make audit risk assessment "easy" and the assurance mission possible

James J. Newhard, CPA
JJN CPA
Paoli, Pennsylvania

Charles dissects one of the most difficult and most misunderstood topics in auditing and renders it easy to understand. He provides a holistic and practical approach to risk assessment. Required reading for all auditors.

Samuel Latimer, CPA, CFE
Rushton and Company, LLC
Gainesville, Georgia

It's easy to look at risk assessment only in terms of what you need to pass peer review. That's a shame because when risk assessment is done well it can laser focus your audits and identify opportunities to help your clients improve their controls. Audit Risk Assessment Made Easy will help you really understand your clients risks and how to respond.

James H. Bennett, CPA, Managing Member
Bennett & Associates, CPAs, PLLC
Ann Arbor, Michigan

The risk assessment part of the audit can sometimes be a neglected part of the audit as it is often misunderstood. Charles does a fantastic job of explaining the importance of the risk assessment process in present day audits and explains it in a way that can be understood by all levels of auditors. Thank you Charles.

Mark A. Welp, CPA, CFE, Principal, Audit & Assurance
Holbrook & Manter, CPAs
Columbus, Ohio

Charles takes the time to explain one of the most difficult aspects of auditing in clear and concise language. His knowledge and wisdom is evident throughout the book with his understanding and enthusiasm providing practical guidance for all levels of auditors. I highly recommend this book for auditors from staff to partner to augment their skills in the crucial area.

Geoff Fulton, CPA, Audit Partner
Fulton and Kozak
Atlanta, Georgia

A general doesn't enter the field of battle without a plan of attack. A coach must devise a plan before taking on an opponent in every sport. Similarly, an auditor cannot embark on an audit without a clear audit plan. The backbone of that plan starts with the risk assessment process. Following the very complex risk assessment standards can be burdensome, confusing, and, in many cases, ripe for opportunities to make a very critical error in the plan that could result in an audit failure. Charles has provided a roadmap to the risk assessment process that is clear, concise, and presented in a way that auditors, both new to the profession and with decades of experience, can follow to ensure their audits are planned appropriately to support their opinion—and pass peer review!

Chris Banta, CPA, CFE, Partner
Brown, Edwards & Company, LLP
Midlothian, Virginia

Charles Hall has made good on his promise to make risk assessment easy. Charles knows his stuff and generously shares his deep knowledge with auditors without putting us all to sleep! His engaging explanations are a pleasure to read.

Leita Hart-Fanta, CPA, CGAP, CGFM
Founder of Yellowbook-CPE.com
Austin, Texas

To my sister, Susan Hall McKinney
Thankful for your love and encouragement throughout my life

Audit Risk Assessment Made Easy
TABLE OF CONTENTS

Introduction xi
Part One: *Risk Assessment Procedures* 1
   Chapter 1 - *Mission Possible: Finding Material Misstatements* 2
   Chapter 2 - *Client Acceptance* 10
   Chapter 3 - *Material Misstatements* 12
   Chapter 4 - *Gaining an Understanding of the Entity and Its Environment* .. 18
   Chapter 5 - *Entity-Level Controls* 22
   Chapter 6 - *Activity-Level Controls* 32
   Chapter 7 - *Walkthroughs* 36
   Chapter 8 - *Override of Controls* 46
   Chapter 9 - *Okay Guys, Any Fraud Here?* 52
   Chapter 10 - *Preliminary Analytical Procedures* 60
   Chapter 11 - *The Close Process* 68
   Chapter 12 - *IT is not ET* 72

Part Two: *Assessing the Risks of Material Misstatement* 77
   Chapter 13 - *The Audit Risk Model* 78
   Chapter 14 - *Relevant Assertions* 82
   Chapter 15 - *Inherent Risk* 90
   Chapter 16 - *Control Risk* 96
   Chapter 17 - *Risks of Material Misstatement* 104

Part Three: *Responses to Risks of Material Misstatement* 109
   Chapter 18 - *Audit Strategy and Plan* 110
   Chapter 19 - *Test of Details* 116
   Chapter 20 - *Substantive Analytics* 120
   Chapter 21 - *Test of Controls* 130
   Chapter 22 - *Three Audit Planning Mistakes* 136

Conclusion 142

INTRODUCTION

Peer review continues to focus on risk assessment. Why? It's the heart and soul of auditing. It's where the battle is won or lost. It's the key to the castle. But sadly, peer review results continue to show that auditors don't understand risk assessment.

The purpose of auditing is to detect material misstatements so we can issue an appropriate audit opinion. If we do this, we carry the day. If we don't, we fail. Knowing how to find material misstatements is our mission. But how?

Seeing What Others Don't

Superman had X-ray vision. He could see things that no one else could because he had a special ability. As auditors, we need a superpower as well: the ability to see material misstatements, wherever they are. Risk assessment gives us that ability. Those who dismiss risk assessment as *something for the peer reviewers* miss this point. Risk assessment *is* your superpower. It's how you see what others miss.

Risk Assessment Reference Book

My goal in writing this book is to provide you with a handy reference book, something you can reach for when you want to grow your superpower. It's short on purpose. So if you are looking for an exhaustive treatise on risk assessment, this is not your book.

My Perspective

I am writing this book from the perspective of an external auditor. My approach and this book are largely influenced by my knowledge of generally accepted auditing standards in the U.S. (GAAS). And how could it not be since I've followed those standards for over thirty-seven years? Though this book is not written specifically for internal auditors, they will find the concepts relevant to their discipline.

Target Audience

Persons who will benefit from this book include:

- External auditors (primary target of this book)
- Internal auditors
- Students preparing to become auditors
- Board members who want to understand auditing

This book provides the nuts and bolts of audit risk assessment. If you're just starting as an auditor, this book is for you. If you've audited for decades, this book is for you. Though the topic is somewhat complex, I've (hopefully) written it in a manner that makes risk assessment understandable and accessible. That's why I've titled it *Audit Risk Assessment Made Easy*.

Audit risk assessment is relevant to every audit in which you issue an opinion based on GAAS. So audit risk assessment is industry-neutral. Use it to audit banks, commercial businesses, nonprofits, governments, and any other industry type.

Common Risk Assessment Questions

This book addresses common questions regarding risk assessment such as:

- Why do I need to understand internal controls if I am using a fully substantive approach?
- What internal controls should I pay attention to?
- What is a walkthrough and when is it needed?
- What risk assessment procedures are required?
- When is an account balance, transaction cycle, or disclosure significant?
- What makes an assertion inherently risky?
- Can I assess control risk at high even though controls are appropriate?
- What is a significant risk?

- How do I assess the risk of material misstatement, including inherent risk and control risk?
- What is linkage and why is it important?
- How do I know what audit procedures to include in my audit programs?

As you read the book, you'll see the answers to these questions and you'll gain a greater ability to see what others miss. In other words, you'll have greater confidence in your ability to understand and use risk assessment. Let me go out on a limb and say that by the time you're done, you just might delight in risk assessment. Is that possible? I'm betting on it.

So let's get started.

PART ONE
Risk Assessment Procedures

CHAPTER 1
Mission Possible: Finding Material Misstatements

As a kid, I loved the T.V. show *Mission Impossible*. The music would start. Trombones, trumpets, flutes playing. And then you would hear the classic line, "Your mission, Jim, should you choose to accept it," and a dangerous goal was given to the team. You knew it was perilous because the message ended with, "If you or any member of your team should be caught or killed, the Secretary will disavow any knowledge of your actions." And then, "in five seconds this message will self-destruct. Good luck, Jim." Heady stuff for an eight-year old.

Auditors have a mission as well. But ours is not impossible, though it may feel like it at times. And thankfully, no one is trying to kill us. But unlike *Mission Impossible*, our goal is always the same. Moreover, the tape does not self-destruct. It just plays over and over again: *Your mission, should you choose to accept it, is to detect material misstatements.*

Material misstatements are the enemy. If they sneak in without detection, we fail. So how do material misstatements enter in? Sometimes they come in by error, and other times on purpose. But regardless, it's your mission to find them, even though they veil themselves in a myriad of places. They could be in receivables, equity, inventory, payables, investments, or a debt disclosure, just to name a few.

When you sign the audit engagement letter, you accept the mission. And if you or any member of your team are caught or killed (that is, you miss material misstatements), the Secretary will not disavow your actions. But he might come looking for you. The Secretary in our world is the AICPA, the state board of accountancy, the General Accounting Office, the Public Company Accounting Oversight Board. Honestly, you'd rather not see these folks. Sure, they're nice people, but it's better to find material misstatements and keep the world safe.

As you audit, you are seeking *reasonable assurance*, not perfect assurance. Perfect assurance costs too much, and it takes too much time. So you're not after perfection. But you do desire, with the time you have, to detect all material misstatements. Otherwise, the words *present fairly* in your audit opinion are not true. It's not your intention to make a false statement. But still, if material misstatements are present, you might opine in error. So, your mission is to find *all* material misstatements.

Risk assessment is the tool that enables you to identify material misstatements. Without it, you are guessing. But with it, you have a means to make your mission possible.

What You're After

You start your audit. And what is before you? Forms, forms, and more forms. Time is passing. Tick, tick, tick. So you dive in. Determined to complete the engagement on time, you roll up your sleeves and ask your client if things are the same as last year. She says yes, and you're relieved. So, what is next?

You think about walkthroughs but decide those can wait. After all, you want to get down to *real* work. So you ask the client for their bank reconciliations and you begin to audit. And why not? This *feels* like auditing. You're thinking, *Just Do It!* Risk assessment can wait. Why? Well, you've done this audit for years. So you know what needs to be done. In short, risk assessment feels like a waste of time. Moreover, nothing ever changes.

But is this true?

One change in controls can lead to millions stolen.

One new accounting person can cause material misstatements.

One new FASB pronouncement can result in key disclosure omissions.

One change in the supply chain can cause significant sales issues.

One related party transaction can mislead users of the financial statements.

One change in strategy can change the business landscape.

I could go on, but I'll spare you.

So even if last year's audit plan was perfect, you need to be aware of current year changes. And how can you do this? Risk assessment.

The purpose of risk assessment is to identify potential material misstatements. And why is that important? Because your goal is to issue an appropriate opinion, most often an unmodified opinion. Such an opinion states that the financial statements are fairly stated, meaning they don't contain material misstatements.

So, again, your mission is to seek out material misstatements, whether they be in the financial statements or the disclosures. This is your target. You want to ensure the reliability of the information. And the financial statement readers are counting on you to do just that.

Hidden Material Misstatements

Even though auditors desire to identify material misstatements, they might stay hidden. Why?

- Risk assessment procedures are not performed
- Risk assessment procedures are performed poorly
- The volume of transactions might hide misstatements
- The complexity of the accounting system makes it difficult to detect errors and fraud
- Identified risks are not placed on the risk assessment summary form
- Team members (with knowledge of risks) move to other engagements
- The multitude and complexity of audit forms create confusion
- Disparate risks are not considered holistically

A Fractured Portrait

It's easy to not see the full risk portrait, especially when there are multiple auditors. Consider the following scenario with Joan, Carl, and Madison as team members:

On April 1, Joan contacts the predecessor auditor and is told that in the year prior, management pushed back on accounts receivable audit entries. And the prior auditors said they were fired, without explanation. But Joan doesn't share this information with Carl prior to his walkthroughs.

On May 3rd, Carl notices that the accounts receivable supervisor handles billing, receipting, and reconciliation of all receivable and revenue accounts. But Carl believes the lack of segregation of duties is offset by the Board's review of monthly financial statements. He is unaware that revenues have risen by 15% annually for the last three years, though the industry is in decline.

On May 10th, Madison creates the planning analytics and observes unusual trends: revenues and receivables increased significantly but the allowance for uncollectibles decreased—at least that's what the general ledger reflects. She notes these changes on her work paper (planning analytics), but makes no mention of them on the risk assessment summary form. The audit team meeting occurs while she is on vacation and the other team members are unaware of her observations. The risk is not considered in planning.

In short, the risk clues are not considered *holistically*. The result is a fractured risk portrait. Though risk clues are documented (they are in the file), the audit team doesn't recognize the potential for fraudulent revenue because there is no composite picture.

Creating a Right Portrait

Risk assessment is similar to drawing a person's portrait. Without a nose, something's missing. It's incomplete. You need the details—eye color, hair style, thickness of lips, ear size, wrinkles, and yes, a nose. Without these, the picture is distorted and incomplete. And not only must these details be known, they must be brought together. Why? So we can see the whole person, the real person. It's the same with risk assessment. The risks of material misstatement portrait enables you to see the real financial statements, whether they are whole and complete, or lacking and incomplete.

And why is this important?

An incomplete risk assessment picture leads to faulty planning. For instance, in the example above, the company appears to record fraudulent receivables and revenue. Yet, the audit team is unaware. Consequently, they don't plan appropriate responses.

Risk assessment leads to accurate pictures, and accurate pictures lead to appropriate responses.

Risk assessment procedures can be thought of as a collection of art tools. After all, we're drawing a picture, are we not? The purpose of those tools is to identify the risks of material misstatement. We do so by:

- Gaining an understanding of the entity and its environment, including internal control, by:
  - Inquiring of client personnel
  - Observing operations and accounting
  - Inspecting client documents
  - Performing walkthroughs of significant transaction cycles
  - Reviewing entity-level controls
  - Inquiring about fraud
  - Understanding the close process
  - Learning about the entity's information technology
- Using planning analytics to see if the numbers appear reasonable
- Creating retrospective reviews of estimates to detect potential bias
- Computing materiality numbers to determine what's important
- Brainstorming about potential risks in an audit team meeting

And as we use these tools, we feed the identified risks to our risk assessment summary document (our picture). As we see unexpected expense changes in the preliminary analytics, we place those on the risk assessment summary form. When we note a lack of segregation of duties in the accounts payable area, we document it on the summary form as well. We continue likewise with other risk assessment procedures, and when we are done, we have a portrait. A work of art! Now we can see the risks of material misstatement clearly.

Next comes our responses.

The Portrait Informs Our Responses

Now we can examine our picture and determine appropriate responses. The portrait informs our planning. And how to we do this?

- We assess risks at the financial statement level
- We develop an overall audit strategy
- We assess risks at the relevant assertion level
- We develop a detailed audit plan

We create our audit plan by linking our risks to our procedures. How? We see a risk and we create a response. The nature of the response is based on the risk. Also, the greater the risk, the greater the response—in terms of procedures (we add more audit steps) and degree (we audit more transactions). If there are no unusual risks, then we might perform our normal audit procedures. For example, in accounts payable, we might perform a search for unrecorded liabilities. But higher risks of material misstatement require more procedures and the testing of more transactions. For example, in the accounts payable area, we might test for double payments to vendors (a fraud scheme whereby employees steal second checks).

Now, let's start our risk assessment process beginning with client acceptance.

Mission Possible: Finding Material Misstatements - A Simple Summary

- The purpose of risk assessment is to identify potential material misstatements so you can plan your audit
- Risk assessment allows auditors to create a risk portrait
- The risk portrait informs the audit plan

CHAPTER 2
Client Acceptance

You get that call you've been waiting for: a potential new audit client; the fee is good as well, and you're elated!

Risk Assessment Starts with Client Acceptance

So you begin the acceptance process: You consider independence, you vet the client for potential problems (can they pay their fee?), and you consider the client's risks of material misstatement. Why? Because risk assessment starts now, not two weeks into the engagement.

As you contact the predecessor auditor, you want to know if there were any accounting disagreements. Did the client pressure the predecessor? Were there passed adjustments? If yes, in what accounts and how much? Were there any control deficiencies?

Additionally, you talk with management. You want to know: does the company plan to incur new debt? Are revenues declining? Are there any inventory issues? Any cash flow problems? Has theft occurred? Have key personnel left?

In short, you are getting a feel for the client's business risk and the client's potential risks of material misstatement. You're surveying management's character and the board's integrity as well. Most importantly, you want to know if they are honest.

Risk assessment starts on day one, even before you accept the client.

Once client acceptance is complete, it's time to begin the audit. And as you do, you'll dig deeper into whether material misstatements are present.

Client Acceptance - A Simple Summary

- Risk assessment starts with the client acceptance process

CHAPTER 3
Material Misstatements

Material misstatements: that's what an auditor looks for. That being the case, let's define materiality and consider its use.

Materiality

Financial statements are seldom perfect. Some misstatements are present, and that's okay as long as they aren't too large. But how large can they be without affecting financial statement users' decisions? Materiality provides the answer. It's a boundary, like white stripes on a basketball court.

That boundary, however, is not constant. The white stripes are different for each audit. Why? Because each entity is different and materiality is judgmental. The boundary is based on what is important to financial statement users. Different users focus on different information.

In one audit, the benchmark is total revenues; in another, it's total assets. The question is, what is a benchmark? It is what's most important to the financial statement users. Once the benchmark is chosen, auditors apply a percent to it to compute materiality—for example, one percent of total assets.

Additionally, qualitative factors play into materiality. Still, auditors need a clearly defined boundary. That's why materiality is number, not a feeling.

So how is materiality defined?

What is Materiality?

The Financial Accounting Standards Board defines materiality as follows:

> *The omission or misstatement of an item in a financial report is material if, in light of surrounding circumstances, the magnitude of the item is such that it is probable that the judgment of a reasonable person relying upon the report would have been changed or influenced by the inclusion or correction of the item.*

Interesting. This definition is not a formula, such as one percent of total assets. Even so, we need clearly laid stripes, do we not? We need a number, even though the auditor considers numbers and narrative information such as notes to the financial statements. We need a number even though materiality is both quantitative and qualitative.

In developing materiality, consider that material misstatements include:

- the omission of a significant disclosure
- an incomplete disclosure
- a known financial statement line misstatement
- an unknown financial statement line misstatement
- an unreasonable estimate

Also, keep in mind that financial statement users—management, owners, lenders, vendors—make decisions. The FASB includes these users in its materiality definition by saying *a reasonable person* whose *judgment...would have changed* if the misstatement were not present. So, what does this *reasonable person* look for? What *omission or misstatement* affects her judgment? And what *magnitude* of misstatement alters her decisions? The answers tell us what materiality is.

Additionally, an entity's risks are important. One business might have a high level of debt, for example. The lender is concerned about debt covenant compliance. Another business has an inventory obsolescence issue. The owners might focus here. Risk impacts materiality for each user.

In light of a myriad of factors, the auditor's job is to provide reasonable assurance that the financial statements are materially correct. So how do we do this? By computing materiality.

Materiality Computation

In order to compute materiality, we must first decide which benchmark is best. Examples include total revenues, total assets, and net income. We select a benchmark that is relevant to financial statement users and stable over time. Often, total assets or total revenues are good choices. So what is a poor example? Net income. Why? Because some businesses "salary out" their profits. Zero net income gives you little to work with. Net income can, however, be appropriate for other entities.

Once the benchmark is selected, we need to apply a percent to compute materiality. The percent is not defined in professional standards, so again, it's judgmental. Most CPAs use percentages in materiality forms provided by third-party publishers; others create their own. Either way, auditors must provide *reasonable assurance* that the financial statements are fairly stated. Therefore, materiality and the related percentages need to be sufficiently low. There are no magical percentages, but an excessively high materiality can lead to an improper audit opinion.

Moreover, materiality is proportional. For instance, a $100,000 error in a billion dollar company may not affect users' decisions. But a $100,000 error in a million dollar company probably would.

Uncorrected and Undetected Misstatements

Even with a good materiality number, uncorrected and undetected misstatements can create problems.

The total of undetected errors may exceed materiality. What if, for example, materiality is $100,000 and there are no uncorrected audit adjustments, but undetected misstatements of $80,000, $20,000, and $25,000 exist in receivables, inventory, and investments, respectively? That would mean an aggregate material misstatement is present.

Similarly, what if materiality is $100,000, the client refuses to post an $80,000 audit adjustment, and there are $45,000 in undetected misstatements? In such a situation, the auditor might *think* the financial statements are fairly stated, but they are not.

Because uncorrected and undetected errors are sometimes material, we need a cushion: a number less than materiality. Something to protect us. And what is that cushion? Performance materiality.

Audit Performance Materiality

Performance materiality is another key to ensuring your audits don't result in improper audit opinions. This number is usually less than overall materiality and applies to transaction classes, account balances, and disclosures.

Performance materiality is a cushion to address the threat that aggregate uncorrected and undetected misstatements might exceed financial statement materiality; that is, overall materiality. Likewise, performance materiality is used at the transaction class, account balance, or disclosure level to ensure that uncorrected and undetected misstatements don't exceed materiality for those areas.

Performance materiality is usually calculated at 50% to 75% of materiality. Why the range? Because there are different risk levels for different clients. If you believe the risk of undetected misstatements is high, then use a lower percent (e.g., 55% of materiality). Likewise, if your client is not inclined to record detected errors, lower the percent. Here is your goal: combined undetected error and uncorrected misstatements must be less than materiality—both for the statements as a whole and for classes of transactions, account balances, and disclosures. We don't want misstatements, in whatever form, to wrongly influence the decisions of financial statement users.

That's why you use performance materiality as you plan your audit procedures for transaction cycles, account balances, and disclosures. For example, if your overall materiality is $1,000,000 and your performance materiality is $750,000, plan your audit procedures for receivables and revenues to ensure there are no misstatements above $750,000.

Uncorrected Misstatements

We need to accumulate uncorrected misstatements in a manner that allows us to judge them at the following levels: classes of transactions, account balances, or disclosures—and the financial statements as a whole.

And this is more than just computing materiality and comparing it to passed adjustments. We should always ask, *Will these uncorrected misstatements adversely affect a user's judgment?* Misstatements caused by fraud, for example, are more significant than those caused by error.

Additionally, consider the effect of uncorrected misstatements from the prior periods.

So what should we document in regard to uncorrected misstatements?

- All known misstatements and whether they were corrected
- A conclusion as to whether uncorrected misstatements are material
- Trivial misstatement amount

Some identified misstatements are so small that they will not be accumulated. We call these trivial misstatements.

Audit Trivial Misstatements

Why create a trivial misstatement amount? Efficiency. All misstatements below the trivial threshold (e.g., $5,000) are not accumulated. The auditor simply notes the trivial difference on the work paper, and she is done. No journal entry is proposed, and no other documentation is necessary. If you expect dozens of trivial amounts, then the trivial threshold should be smaller. You don't want the cumulative trivial misstatements to become material.

Material Misstatement - A Simple Summary

- To find material misstatements, we must know what materiality is
- Materiality includes omissions or misstatements that adversely affect the judgment of financial statement users
- Auditors compute a materiality dollar amount, usually a percent of a benchmark, such as total revenues
- Performance materiality is used in planning audit responses for account balances, transaction cycles, and disclosures
- Performance materiality is usually a percent of overall materiality and acts as a cushion in case undetected misstatements are present
- Undetected misstatements can lead to improper opinions
- Uncorrected audit entries (those not posted by the client) are summarized and evaluated by the auditor to see if they are material
- Trivial misstatements are differences passed at the work paper level with no proposed audit adjustments

CHAPTER 4
Gaining an Understanding of the Entity and Its Environment

Auditors should obtain an understanding of the entity and its environment.

Business Risk

In order to understand the risk of material misstatement, we need to understand business risk. But what is business risk? It's the risk that a company will not meet its objectives. For example, the company might desire to make a profit of $1 million in the current year. The business risk is that they will fail to do so.

So, why do auditors need to understand business objectives and risks? Because they affect the risk of material misstatement. Suppose the CEO's compensation is tied to a company objective (e.g., $1 million in profit). That might mean management would manipulate the numbers, causing a fraud risk.

Sometimes we think of business risk as something particular to commercial entities, but nonprofits and governments have this risk as well. Suppose a nonprofit has a goal of securing a large grant. But grant acceptance is dependent upon meeting certain criteria, such as feeding five thousand homeless persons. With such a grant the nonprofit might inflate its feeding statistics. Why? To receive the money. After all, it has a mission to feed the poor, and it can't do so without funds. As you can see, even a well-intended goal can lead to fraud.

Regardless of the entity type—for-profit, nonprofit, governmental—auditors need to be aware of objectives. We need to step into the shoes of those who manage or govern the entity. Go ahead: sit down in the CEO's chair. Consider what she desires. Also, look at the business from the board's perspective. What are they expecting?

Understanding business risk sheds light on the heartbeat of the organization. And when you understand the business, you'll better understand the numbers and the possibility of fraud. You may be thinking, *But it's cynical to imply that fraud might be present.* While I don't desire to consider fraud (my mother taught me to trust others), it is my responsibility to exercise professional skepticism. It's central to what we do. We question in order to see what *could* happen given the dynamics of the entity.

General Information

What else do you need to know?

- Who the competitors are
- If there are any related party transactions
- The composition and amounts of significant assets, liabilities, revenues, expenses
- Whether the company is subject to regulatory oversight
- The nature of the industry and any changes therein
- New accounting standards affecting the entity
- Key customers and suppliers
- Whether there are any debt covenants
- How often the board meets and what they focus on
- Whether there are any going concern issues
- What the key ratios are
- Whether there are any legal problems
- What the legal structure is (e.g., LLC, corporation) and whether the entity pays taxes

- The key benefits offered to employees such as pensions, bonuses, stock options
- The reporting framework (e.g., GAAP)

Entity Characteristics

Each entity has its own personality. Nonprofits are usually dependent upon contributions, governments upon taxes, and businesses upon sales. Commercial entities may offer bonuses; governments may not. One entity is highly leveraged; another is not. A government has elected officials; a public company, board members. A commercial business pays out owner distributions; a nonprofit has no owners. One business pays taxes; another is a passthrough entity. One company operates in a declining industry; another in an emerging one.

So each entity has its own ecosystem, and when you understand it, you're in a better position to audit. But a lack of understanding may lead to undetected material misstatements.

Open-Ended Questions

So how can you ferret out the most important information? Use open-ended questions with key personnel or board members such as:

- If you could wave a magic wand over the business and change three things, what would those be?
- What keeps you awake at night?
- If you owned the entire business, what would you change?

Open-ended questions regarding that which affects emotions—the people you are working with are humans, after all—tap into what is of greatest concern.

Once you know what the important factors are, ask yourself, *How does this affect the possibility of material misstatements?* Then bring that information into your risk assessment summary.

Another important risk assessment tool is understanding the system of internal control. The system is made up of entity-level controls (addressed in the next chapter) and activity-level controls (addressed two chapters hereafter).

Gaining an Understanding of the Entity and Its Environment - A Simple Summary

- Auditors must understand the entity and its environment to know where material misstatements might occur
- Business risk affects the potential for material misstatements
- Business risk exists for all types of entities including nonprofits and governments
- Auditors need to understand entity characteristics such as competition, the amount of debt, key customers and suppliers, and the industry
- Use open-ended questions to gain a better understanding of the entity

CHAPTER 5
Entity-Level Controls

Activity-level controls—those such as segregation of duties—get all the love. Entity-level controls, on the other hand, are the red-headed stepchild; many times they don't receive the attention and respect they deserve. But we need to understand the *full* system of internal control.

COSO

The fountainhead of internal controls is *Internal Control - Integrated Framework*, as provided by the Committee of Sponsoring Organizations (COSO). Auditors recognize the COSO control components when they see:

1. Control environment
2. Risk assessment
3. Monitoring
4. Information and communication
5. Control activities

Consideration of these components is necessary to understand any entity's system of internal controls.

Scalable Internal Controls

The five components, when designed and working correctly, result in materially correct financial statements. In larger businesses, the five components are often more clearly defined. Smaller entities, by contrast, tend to blend the five components, making them less distinct. Regardless, the entity-level and activity-level controls are important in *all* companies, nonprofits, and governments.

The system of internal control is scalable. Larger and more complex entities normally have extensive controls, while smaller and less complex entities usually have fewer controls. Consequently, the auditor's internal control documentation is scalable as well. There is no one-size-fits-all system of internal control. Therefore, the auditor's internal control documentation varies in length and content, based on the entity being audited.

Design and Implementation of Controls

Whether you are examining entity-level or activity-level controls, consider the design and implementation of controls. Auditors tend to pay more attention to design and implementation as they relate to activity-level controls, but they are equally important for entity-level controls. The design of controls, especially the entity-level controls, can be less distinct in smaller businesses than those of larger entities. So reviewing the appropriateness of entity-level controls for these entities can be challenging. Even so, understanding entity-level controls is important.

Control Environment

The first entity-level control is control environment, which many refer to as *tone at the top*. In examining this component, ask questions about those charged with governance and management. Are they committed to accurate financial statement reporting? Do they receive internal control reports? If the entity has internal auditors, how often do they meet with the board? If there are no internal auditors, how receptive is the board to external audit communications regarding internal controls?

The control environment component is more subjective than the other four. Therefore, testing for appropriate design and implementation is more challenging. So, what should you look for? What documents should you review?

Some companies have a code of conduct. If they do, review it and see if company personnel are familiar with it. Is the code a part of the company's DNA or just a document in the filing cabinet?

In all entities, see if the board members and management actively govern. Read the minutes to understand the board's participation level. Review board reports and see how often they receive these and whether they understand them.

How often does the board or the owners meet? If monthly, great. If once a year, not so good.

Is there a conflict-of-interest statement and does the company abide by it? Do board members and management disclose their potential conflicts annually?

Does the entity have a whistle-blower policy? Can employees anonymously report suspicious activity? Who receives the whistle-blower reports? Who follows up on them and how often? How does the company respond to theft?

If the company has internal auditors, do they report directly to the board or to management? Internal auditors should have a *direct* line to those charged with governance. Additionally, internal auditors should be hired and fired by the board, not management. Why? Because internal auditors monitor the actions of management.

Are appropriate resources given to information technology (IT) personnel? Does IT provide periodic operating reports to the board and management? Do they have sufficient education and knowledge? What is IT doing to protect the information system? Is IT accountable to leadership? Are they transparent about their activities?

And what about management personnel? Are they accountable to the board? In some organizations, the chief executive officer (CEO) runs the company with little accountability. This is not desirable in larger entities, but quite common and maybe necessary in smaller ones. The CEO and an owner might be one and the same in a smaller business.

Honesty is the key to the control environment. And honesty is not what the leadership says, but what it does. So ask yourself, *Do they walk the talk?* Hopefully, you see integrity and transparency.

Even though the control environment is more subjective than the other four components, review the design and implementation of these controls when possible. You can only do so with controls, not personal characteristics. You can't review the CEO's ethics, for example, but you can read the code of conduct. You can't review the CFO's transparency, but you can examine a whistle-blower program. You can't review board chair's intelligence, but you can inspect monthly financial statements as provided to the board. Look for controls, not just subjective characteristics. Asking, *Are your board members ethical?* is not enough.

But what if there are no control environment documents such as a code of conduct? In smaller entities this is possible, though most organizations provide financial reports to those in charge. If there are no controls, consider the impact on the risk of material misstatement. Also, consider whether compensating controls exist in the other four components of the internal control system.

Now, let's look at another entity-level control: risk assessment.

Risk Assessment

Examine the design and implementation of the risk assessment component. This can be challenging in smaller entities with no formal risk assessment process. Even so, risk assessment controls are often still present.

For example, a small business owner's risk assessment process might include financial statement reviews. Since she knows her business well, errant numbers are detectable. Moreover, she considers the competency of her accountants, knowing that smart accountants lead to good numbers. Additionally, she hires outside IT professionals to maintain the information system, or she uses cloud-based software such as QuickBooks. Why? IT is a part of a healthy accounting system. So as you can see, small business risk assessment can be informal, yet still effective.

In larger companies, risk assessment is more robust. The board and management periodically meet to focus on risk assessment, and these meetings are documented. Additionally, internal auditors might test the accounting system and provide reports to leadership. Consequently, it's easier to review risk assessment design and implementation in such an environment.

Regardless of the entity size, companies normally use disclosure checklists to prepare their financial statements, and such checklists lower the risk of incomplete or omitted disclosures.

Does the company present consolidated financial statements? Then consolidating controls, such as a second-person review, are necessary. Improper consolidating procedures can easily result in material misstatements. Therefore, risk assessment should encompass the consolidation process.

Most importantly, company personnel should think about how the financial statements might contain material misstatements in light of the existing controls, accounting personnel, and business dynamics. So, has anyone considered how errors or fraud might occur? And is the risk assessment process documented? If yes, then the auditor should review it. If no, then the auditor should consider the company's informal processes and whether they decrease the risk of material misstatements.

Risk assessment works best when monitoring reports are used by the organization. So let's consider another entity-level control: monitoring.

Monitoring

Errors and fraud can occur even when a company has a great internal control structure. Therefore, monitoring is necessary to detect misstatements.

As we said in the risk assessment section, larger companies often have internal auditors. And those auditors provide reports to the board and management about financial reporting, whether it is occurring properly or not. Such interim monitoring lessens the probability of material misstatements by timely identifying misstatements and correcting them as they occur.

But even if an organization has no internal auditors, monitoring can still occur. The CFO can review monthly accounting reports. The payroll supervisor can compare the current compensation reports with earlier ones. The board can review budget-to-actual reports. The owner can compare production statistics with monthly financial statements.

Segregation of duties—which is an activity-level control—may be lacking, especially in smaller organizations. However, the board or owners might choose to review monthly financial statements as a compensating control. While the financial statement review is a high-level control (and usually not as effective as segregation of duties), it can lower the risk of misstatement. Additionally, in entities with budgets, the board might receive budget-to-actual reports. Moreover, the board could review a list of disbursements.

Vetting the design and implementation of monitoring is usually much easier than reviewing the control environment or risk assessment. Why? Well, monitoring requires reports that can be reviewed by the external auditor. In other words, monitoring reports provide the auditor with physical or electronic evidence of controls.

If the monitoring reports enable the organization to detect and correct material misstatements, then this component is properly *designed*. And companies that generate and review monitoring reports have *implemented* the control. But if monitoring reports are not present, a control weakness might exist.

Creating monitoring reports is a part of another entity-level control: information and communication.

Information and Communication

As you consider information and communication, ask questions such as:

- How does the entity communicate its internal controls?
- How does a company inform its employees about the financial reporting process?
- Do training manuals exist?
- Are internal controls mapped in a flowchart?
- What reports are provided to the board and management, or to an owner of the company?
- Are dashboards used?
- How are errors communicated and corrected?

Most smaller entities communicate the internal control structure verbally. A new person is hired and the supervisor explains what is to be done. And often times the supervisor knows what to say because the same was explained to her on the day she was hired. Similar to control environment and risk assessment, the information and communication component is not always clearly defined in smaller organizations. By contrast, larger entities tend to have more formal internal control or accounting manuals: these policies are stated in black and white. But either way—whether verbal or in writing—the bottom line is whether the control structure is properly communicated.

When internal controls are communicated verbally, the auditor needs to ask employees how they learned about the accounting system and related internal controls. Then the auditor should observe the daily operations to see if the controls are properly performed.

When the internal controls are communicated in writing, the auditor should review the guidance. And again, they should observe the organization's personnel to see if they understand the accounting system and controls.

Regarding information and communication, you want to know if the accounting handbooks, internal control reports, and financial reports lessen the probability of material misstatement. Does everyone know their internal control responsibilities? Are reports provided in a timely manner? If there is a breakdown in the controls, is that information communicated to those who can mend the weakness?

Entity-Level Controls

My purpose in writing this chapter is to remind you of the importance of entity-level controls. Give them a little love and respect. Pay attention to them. In some ways, they are more important than activity-level controls. After all, if the board and management aren't honest, what good are activity-level controls? And even if the leadership is honest, risk assessment is necessary to detect breakdowns in the control structure. Monitoring, as a sister to risk assessment, will help the company see control weaknesses in a timely manner. Additionally, information and communication makes everyone aware of their internal control responsibilities.

In a perfectly designed internal control system, each component complements and supports the other, making the risk of material misstatement less likely. Lower risk means fewer substantive procedures and test of controls, but higher risk means more work for the auditor. Significant entity-level control weaknesses should be documented on the risk assessment summary form.

Next, we will dig a little deeper into understanding internal controls by looking at activity-level controls.

Entity Level Controls - A Simple Summary

- COSO is the fountainhead of internal controls
- Internal controls are scalable based on the size and complexity of an entity
- Auditors examine the design and implementation of controls at the entity-level and activity-level
- Control environment is the tone at the top and can include controls such as a code of conduct, conflict-of-interest statements, and whistle-blower programs
- Entities should perform risk assessment procedures to determine how misstatements might occur
- Entities should monitor controls and financial reporting since errors or fraud can occur
- Clear information and communication processes enhance the system of internal controls and financial accounting
- Weaknesses in entity-level controls should be documented on the risk assessment summary form

CHAPTER 6
Activity-Level Controls

Internal controls (also called the system of internal control) prevent material misstatements. But, as we discussed in the Entity-Level Control chapter, two things must be present in the system of internal controls: proper design and implementation.

Design of Controls

First, consider design. Suppose your business allows the accounts payable clerk, the nephew of the owner, to make electronic vendor payments. Furthermore, this same person is solely responsible for setting up new vendors in the payable software. While monthly payments are around $10 million, the only internal control is the owner's review of the monthly financial statements. This control is a poor one. Why? Because the clerk could easily create and send electronic payments to a fictitious vendor, whereby stealing money without detection. The control, the owner's review of the financial statements, would probably not uncover or prevent thefts. Though a control is present, the design is weak.

In designing internal controls, companies should ask, *What can go wrong?* For instance, if new vendors are not vetted, what can happen? Funds can be paid to a fictitious vendor. If true, then how can the company lessen that threat? It could implement a vendor review process, one performed by someone other than the person setting up the vendor.

Control design is challenging, however. Why? Because there

are multiple ways to improve controls. In the example above, an additional control could be added: the CFO could review all new vendors on a daily basis. Alternatively, the owner could review new vendors every two weeks. Or the company could hire an external CPA to vet new vendors on a surprise basis. No one solution exists and some solutions are better than others. Good design—in this example—results in the prevention of fictitious vendors. So as the company designs the control, it should consider which option meets that goal with the least amount of effort and cost.

Implementation of Controls

Second, consider implementation of controls. Suppose a new control is added: all new vendors are to be reviewed and approved by the owner. But the owner, because she's too busy, doesn't perform the control. Creating a control and intending to perform it is not enough. It has to be implemented. What good is a control if it is not in use?

Understanding Controls

Because control solutions are many, auditors must understand accounting systems and what can go wrong.

For example, what can go wrong with cash collections? Someone could steal incoming cash. So what can the company do to reduce the theft of cash? It can perform daily reconciliations of the cash drawer activity, reconciling the cash received with that which is recorded in the receipting software. Thereafter, the cash receipts supervisor could review this reconciliation.

In another example, what can go wrong in inventory? Ordered inventory could be shipped to the wrong location. To mitigate this risk, someone could reconcile the ordered inventory with received inventory.

And in another example, what can go wrong with accounts payable? Invoices might be received in the mail but not keyed into the accounts payable system. To address this risk, the payables supervisor could review the invoices to see if they have been entered.

What is a Control?

We've been discussing the importance of controls, but we need to know: what constitutes a control?

It's an action performed to lessen the possibility of misstatement (whether by error or fraud) in the accounting system.

In the three examples just provided, the control is not the collection of cash or the physical receipt of inventory or the opening of mail for invoices. Controls are those actions taken to ensure that the accounting is correct and that fraud is not occurring, such as reviewing the daily cash drawer activity, reconciling ordered inventory, and reviewing vendor invoices to see if they have been recorded.

As the auditor, you want to know if the controls mitigate the risk of material misstatement, that they are *designed* correctly and that they are *implemented*. If they are, then the system is sound. If not, then material misstatements can occur.

Small Entity Controls

One common peer review comment is that auditors don't document internal controls for small entities. These auditors say there are no controls. All entities, however, have *some* controls and those controls should be documented in the audit work papers. Here are examples of small entity controls:

- Reconciliation of monthly bank statements
- Reconciliation of receivables and payables to the general ledger

- Customer checks are stamped *For Deposit Only*
- Use of software passwords
- Inventory is maintained in a secure location
- Use of security cameras
- Management reviews payroll reports from external payroll companies
- Owners review the monthly financial statements
- Review of aged receivables
- Restriction of authorized check signers to one or two people
- Check stock is kept in a secure location
- Monthly budget-to-actual reports are reviewed
- Online bank account activity is viewable by the owner

I am not saying these limited controls are sufficient, but even so, auditors should document the controls that exist. The presence or lack of controls can impact your control risk assessment (I'll explain more in the Control Risk chapter). Key activity-level control weaknesses should be noted on the risk assessment summary form.

You as the auditor need to understand the system of internal control. But how? Walkthroughs, the topic of the next chapter.

Control Activities - A Simple Summary

- Auditors use walkthroughs to review the design and implementation of activity-level controls
- Activity-level control weaknesses can lead to risks of material misstatement; such weaknesses should be noted on the risk assessment summary form
- A control is an action performed to lessen the possibility of misstatements, whether by error or fraud
- All entities, even small ones, have internal controls and these should be documented for significant transaction areas

CHAPTER 7
Walkthroughs

What is a walkthrough? It's taking a transaction *through* the accounting system to see if controls are appropriately designed and in use. As you perform the walkthrough, you ask yourself *What can go wrong? Can someone steal? Can mistakes occur?* You want to know if there is a risk of material misstatement.

Walkthroughs are primarily performed in regard to transaction cycles such as billing and collection.

To understand walkthroughs, we need to answer these questions:
- What is a walkthrough?
- What is the purpose of a walkthrough?
- How can auditors document walkthroughs?
- Is it best to use checklists, flowcharts, or to summarize controls narratively?
- How often should walkthroughs be performed?
- Are walkthroughs required?
- Will a walkthrough allow me to assess control risk at less than high?

What are Audit Walkthroughs?

Walkthroughs are cradle-to-grave reviews of transaction cycles. You start at the beginning of a transaction cycle (usually a source document) and walk the transaction to the end (usually a posting to the general ledger). The auditor is gaining an understanding of not only how a transaction makes its way through the accounting system, but more importantly, what the related controls are.

As we perform a walkthrough, we:
- Make inquiries
- Inspect documents
- Make observations

By asking questions, inspecting documents, and making observations, we evaluate internal controls to see if control weaknesses could allow errors or fraud to occur. Audit standards do not permit the use of inquiries alone. So, we observe people and their actions, and we inspect documents: we *see* the accounting system in action.

Some auditors believe that audit walkthroughs (or documentation of controls for significant transaction cycles) are not necessary if the auditor is assessing control risk at high, but this is not true. While the auditor can assess control risk at high, she must first gain an understanding of the cycle and the related controls. In other words, the auditor can't default to high and skip risk assessment.

What an Audit Walkthrough is Not

Following a transaction through the accounting system–without reviewing controls–is not an audit walkthrough. For example, knowing that check number 3458 was posted to the general ledger does not tell us about controls. Knowing that Bill signed the check and that John entered the transaction into the system does. Remember, we examine controls to see if they are properly designed and to see if they have been implemented. This is the purpose of the walkthrough. If we don't gain an understanding of controls, then we can't determine their effects upon the risk of material misstatement. Sound internal controls lower risk. Weak internal controls, on the other hand, increase risk.

Placing a copy of the operating and accounting manual in the audit file is not a walkthrough. While manuals tell us what the client *should* do, they don't tell us what the client *is* doing. In other words, they don't answer the implementation question.

Also, asking a client, *Is everything the same as last year?* is not a walkthrough. Auditors must do more than inquire. They must inspect documents and observe controls in action.

Internal Controls Documented in Prior Audits

In some situations, auditors rely on audit evidence obtained in prior periods. When they do, auditors must perform audit procedures to establish the continued relevance of the audit evidence obtained in those periods.

It's fine to roll forward your previous year's walkthroughs to the current year, but re-perform and update those procedures in the current year to determine if controls have changed. We must do so annually—before we plan the audit—to see if the controls are still designed appropriately and to see if they are still in use.

Suppose in the prior year that Dorothy Hardin (and no one else) could add new vendors to the payables system. But now Dorothy and a new guy, Gary Collins, can do so. Additionally, Gary signs checks and reconciles the bank statement. During the year, he steals $300,000—and no one knows it. Without updating our understanding of controls, we are unaware of the system's weakness. The result: we don't identify a risk of material misstatement, and no audit procedures are planned as a response.

You may be wondering if current walkthroughs provide a basis for assessing control risk at less than high. In other words, is a walkthrough considered a test of controls?

Walkthroughs and Lower Control Risk Assessment

Usually, audit walkthroughs are not sufficient to support lower control risk assessments (those less than high). If the auditor assesses control risk at less than high, she is required to test the effectiveness of the control. Since audit walkthroughs are usually a test of one transaction, they typically don't prove operating *effectiveness*.

An auditor can determine whether a control is properly designed and is in use by testing one transaction. For example, the auditor might look at one purchase order to see if this control is in place. Effectiveness, on the other hand, usually requires a test of transactions, such as the examination of sixty purchase orders. Because a test of controls is often necessary to assess control risk at less than high, auditors often assess control risk at high as an *efficiency* decision (the auditor believes substantive procedures will take less time than the control testing). That way, the test of sixty purchase orders is avoided. But if a test of controls is not performed, the auditor must perform substantive procedures when a risk of material misstatement is present.

Audit Walkthrough Documentation

While you can use checklists, flowcharts, narratives, or any other method to document your understanding of controls, my favorite is a narrative mixed with screenshots.

So how do I do this?

I interview personnel regarding transaction cycle internal controls. Usually, one or two people can explain a particular transaction flow (e.g., disbursement cycle), but some complicated processes may require several interviews.

Early on, I may not know how each person's work fits into the complete picture; that makes it like gathering puzzle pieces. The interviews and information can feel random, even confusing. But later, when I put the parts together, the picture speaks clearly (if not, I ask more questions). Now I understand the accounting system and control environment.

My Audit Walkthrough Tools

I document the conversations using:

- A writing instrument that also captures audio (e.g., Livescribe)
- My iPhone camera

Taking Notes

Using a Livescribe pen, I write notes and record the conversations. I sometimes, alternatively, use an app such as Notability with my iPad. This app records audio as I take notes on my iPad screen.

I remind myself of the purpose of the interview: to understand the internal controls. Then I begin the interview by saying, *Tell me what you do and how you do it. Treat me as if I know nothing. I want to hear all the details.*

As I listen, I write notes. At the same time, my Livescribe pen records the audio. Later, the conversation can be played from the pen.

I find that most interviewees talk too fast—at least faster than I can write. As I'm writing about the last thing I've heard, they are moving to the next, and I fall behind. So I write simple phrases in my Livescribe notebook such as:

- Add vendor
- Charlie opens mail
- P.O. issued by Purchasing
- Checks signed by the computer

Later, as I'm typing the narrative, I touch the letter *A* in *Add vendor* with the tip of my Livescribe pen. This action causes the pen to play the audio for that part of the conversation. Likewise, touching C in *Checks signed by the computer* causes the pen to play that part of the conversation. Since the audio syncs with my notes, I can hear any part of the discussion by touching a letter with my pen. (The Notability iPad app, if used in place of the Livescribe pen, does the same.)

Taking Pictures

In addition to writing notes in my Livescribe notebook, I take pictures with my iPhone. Here are examples (these are from a payables interview):

- Invoice with approver's initials
- Screenshot of an invoice entry
- If there are multiple payable clerks, a picture of the team
- A signed check
- A bank reconciliation

So my inputs into the walkthrough document are as follows:

- Livescribe notes and audio
- Photos of documents and persons

Audit Walkthrough Summary

I write my description of the system and controls in Word and embed pictures as needed. The walkthrough documentation takes this shape:

- Narrative
- Pictures
- Key control identification
- Control weakness identification (if any)

The narrative includes information such as the software used, the number of people in the department, who those people are, their years of service, who the supervisor is, whether surprise tests are made, problem areas during the year, and internal controls. The key is the documentation of controls, but the other information provides context. I am careful, however, not to include too much contextual information. Why? Too much background information can obscure the control information.

While pictures are not required, they illuminate your understanding of internal control design and operation. Pictures aid my understanding in the current year, but more importantly, pictures aid my recall in the following year. After all, a picture is worth a thousand words.

Another key feature of the walkthrough documentation is the identification of who I spoke with and when. So, at the top of the transaction cycle description, I name the persons I interview and the date of the conversation. For example:

> *Charles Hall interviewed Johnny Mann, Hector Nunez, and Suzanne Milton, the accounts payable personnel, on October 25, 20XX.*

Some controls are not key controls; in other words, they don't significantly decrease the risk of material misstatement. It's fine to document these lesser controls, but it's more important to identify the key ones. I do so by typing *Key Control* with bolded font.

For example:

> **Key Control:** *Additions of new vendors is limited to two persons in the accounts payable department. Each day the accounts payable software automatically provides the CFO with a new vendor list. The CFO reviews that list for appropriateness. Persons adding new vendors cannot process signed checks.*

Once I complete the narrative, I step back and review the key controls to see if there are any control weaknesses. I ask myself, *in light of the key controls, is there a control weakness?* If there is, I note it, using a bolded font.

For example:

> **Control Weakness:** *Only one signature is required for check disbursements. Johnny Mann signs checks, has possession of check stock, keys invoices into the payables system, and reconciles the related bank account.*

Why identify control deficiencies? So I can include them in my risk assessment summary. Additionally, highlighting control weaknesses makes it easy to locate them when I write my internal control letter (the letter that communicates significant deficiencies and material weaknesses) to the client.

Response to Risk of Material Misstatement

In the example above, the control weakness created by Johnny Mann's duties increases the risk of theft. I note this risk on my risk assessment summary form. What is my response? I establish audit procedures in my audit program to address the risk, such as:

- Review one month's cleared checks for appropriate payees

How do you know what to do in response to a risk? Ask, *What can go wrong?* and design a test for that potential. Johnny can write checks to himself. My response? Scan cleared checks to see if any are made out to him.

Look Beyond the Normal Client Procedures

It's easy for clients to tell you about *normal* procedures, but they may not think about *unusual* situations such as the absence of an employee or how errors are corrected. You want to understand the workarounds.

Ask who performs control procedures when a key person is out. Why? If someone can—even though he normally doesn't—

perform accounting functions, you need to know this. For example, if a person does not normally issue signed checks but can, and that person also reconciles the bank statement, he might create fraudulent checks. He knows the theft will not be detected through the normal internal controls—in this case, the bank reconciliation.

Look beyond accounting policies and routine procedures to see what can happen. Clients sometimes make statements such as *John is the only one who approves the purchase orders.* But I know this is not true because purchases would cease if John were out. So I ask, *Who issues purchase orders when John is on vacation?*

Additionally, ask how errors are corrected. When things go wrong, you want to know how they are made right. The workaround might be a control weakness, a bypassing of normal controls.

Walkthroughs in Complex Environments

For most small businesses, performing a walkthrough is not that hard. Pick a transaction cycle; start at the beginning and follow the transaction to the end.

In more complex companies, break the transaction cycle into pieces. You know the old question, *How do you eat an elephant?* And the answer, *One bite at a time.* So, the process for understanding smaller companies works for a larger ones as well. Just break it down and allow more time.

Even when great controls are in place, management can override them. We will consider that threat next.

Walkthroughs - A Simple Summary

- Walkthroughs are a key risk assessment procedure and should be performed annually
- Walkthroughs include inquiries, inspection, and observations

for significant transaction cycles
- Walkthroughs generally do not provide a basis for lower control risk assessment
- Walkthroughs provide initial impressions of internal controls, but a test of controls is necessary to vet the effectiveness of those controls (if control risk is to be assessed below high)
- Document key controls, those that prevent or detect material misstatements
- Documentation of walkthroughs can include narratives, checklists, flowcharts, or other methods
- Consider using an audio recording device and a camera as you perform walkthroughs
- Be clear in documenting internal control weaknesses
- Place control weaknesses on the risk assessment summary form if they might allow material misstatements

CHAPTER 8
Override of Controls

Controls can be overridden, even when properly designed and operating. Accounting personnel often comply with the wishes of management either out of loyalty or fear. So if a trusted C.E.O. asks the accounting staff to perform questionable actions, they will sometimes comply because they trust the leader. Also, management can threaten accounting personnel with the loss of their jobs if they don't comply with their demands. Either way, management gets its way by overriding internal controls.

Four Ways to Override Controls

Here are four examples of how management can override controls:

1. Booking journal entries to inflate profits or cover up theft
2. Using significant transactions outside the normal course of business to dress up the financial statements
3. Manipulating estimates
4. Transferring company cash to personal accounts

Auditors consider management override in all audits (or at least, they should). Why? Because it's always possible.

First, let's consider how management overrides controls with journal entries.

Journal Entry Fraud

Think about the WorldCom fraud. Expenses were capitalized to inflate profits. Income statement amounts were moved to the balance sheet with questionable entries. When the fraud was discovered, the internal auditors were told the billion-dollar entries were *based on what management wanted*. The entries were not in accordance with generally accepted accounting principles. And why was this done? To increase stock prices. Management owned shares of WorldCom, so they profited from the sale of inflated stock prices. The fraud led to prison sentences and the demise of the company, all because of management override.

Journal entries are an easy way to override controls. Consider this scenario: management meets at year-end, and they have not met their goals; so they manipulate earnings by recording nonexistent receivables and revenues, or they record revenues before they are earned. For example, management accrues $10 million in fake revenue, or they move January revenues (from the subsequent year) to December (in the current year).

Auditors should test journal entries for potential fraud, but how? First, understand the normal process for making journal entries: learn who makes them, when are they made, and how. Also, inquire about journal entry controls and consider any fraud incentives, such as bonuses related to profits. Then think about where fraudulent entries might be made and test those accounts. Fraudulent journal entries are often made at year-end, so make sure you test those. Here are some additional ideas for testing journal entries:

- Review nonstandard entries
- Examine entries made to seldom-used accounts
- Review consolidating entries (also known as top-side entries)
- Test entries made at unusual hours (e.g., during the night)

- Vet entries made by persons that don't normally make journal entries
- Look at suspense account entries
- Review round-dollar entries (e.g., $100,000)

You don't need to perform all of the above tests, just the ones that are higher risk in light of journal entry controls and fraud incentives. Data mining software can help in vetting journal entries. For example, you can search for journal entries made by unauthorized persons. Just extract all journal entries from the general ledger and group them by persons making the entries; afterward, scan the list for unauthorized persons.

Fraudulent journal entries are not the only way to override controls. The books can be cooked with related party transactions.

Funny Business

Sometimes, as an auditor, you'll see funny transactions. No, I don't mean they are amusing. I mean they are *unusual*. Management can alter profits with transactions *outside the normal course of business*, and these are often related party transactions.

Burning Fire, an audit client, is owned by Don Jackson. Mr. Jackson also owns another business, Placid Lake. As you are auditing Burning Fire, you see it received a check for $10 million dollars from Placid Lake. So you ask for transaction support, but there is little. The CFO says the payment was made for *prior services rendered*, but it doesn't ring true. This could be fraud and is an example of a transaction outside the normal course of business. Why would a company record such an entry? Possibly to bolster Burning Fire's financial statements. When you see such a transaction, consider whether there is a fraud incentive. For example, do loan covenants require certain financial ratios and does this transaction bring them into compliance?

Next, we will look at how management can juice up profits by manipulating estimates.

Manipulating Estimates

Auditing standards require a retrospective review of estimates as a risk assessment procedure. Why? Because management can manipulate estimates to inflate earnings and assets. Audit standards call such tendencies *bias,* a sign that fraudulent financial reporting might exist. That's why auditors review prior estimates and related results.

For instance, suppose a company has a policy of reserving 90% of receivables that are ninety days or older. If at year-end the greater-than-ninety-days bucket contains $1,000,000, management can increase earnings $400,000 by lowering the reserve to 50%. What an easy way to increase net income!

So, how does an auditor perform a retrospective review of an allowance for uncollectible accounts? Review the prior year allowances by examining bad debts recorded thereafter. If allowances were understated in prior years, bias might exist. Then compare the current year reserve with that of the last two or three years. If the reserve decreases, ask why. There might be legitimate reasons for the decline. But if there is no reasonable basis for the smaller allowance, fraud could be present. Note such changes on your risk assessment summary form. For example, in the accounts receivable section, you might say: *The allowance for uncollectible accounts appears to have decreased without a reasonable basis.* Why note this on the form? Because you've identified a fraud risk that deserves attention.

Complex estimates are easier to manipulate without detection than simple ones. Why? Because intricate estimates are harder to understand and complexity creates a smokescreen, making bias more difficult to spot. As an example, consider pension plan assumptions and estimates; they are very complex. And changes in the assumptions can dramatically affect the balance sheet and net income.

Document your retrospective review. You can accomplish this by listing the current and prior year estimates and explain the basis for each. Also, examine the results of the prior year estimates. For example, compare the current year bad debts with the prior year uncollectible allowance. Additionally, consider including incentives for manipulating profits such as bonuses.

Label the work paper *Retrospective Review of Estimates* to communicate its purpose. **Also, consider adding purpose and conclusion statements such as:**

Purpose of work paper: To perform a retrospective review of estimates to see if bias is present.

Conclusion: While the allowance estimate is higher in the current year, the judgments and assumptions are the same. It does not appear that bias is present. All other prior year estimates appear reasonable.

Other conclusion examples follow:

Conclusion: The rate of return used in computing the pension liability increased by 1%. The increase does not appear to be warranted given the mix of investments and past history. Bias appears to be present and is noted in the risk assessment summary form (in the payroll and benefits section).

Conclusion: Based on our review of the economic lives of assets in the prior year depreciation schedule, no bias is noted.

Conclusion: We reviewed bad debt write-offs in the current year and compared them to the uncollectible allowance in the prior year. No management bias is noted.

Is there another way that management might override controls? Yes, sometimes management requires accounting personnel to transfer company cash to personal bank accounts.

Transferring Company Cash to Personal Accounts

Years ago I audited a hospital in Alabama. The C.E.O. would sometimes go to Panama City Beach, and while there, direct his accounting staff to wire funds to his personal account—and they did. Why? They were threatened with job loss. Some management personnel, especially those with muscle, can intimidate the accounting employees into doing the unbelievable. I've seen this happen, and when the C.E.O. is called out, he pleads ignorance about prior conversations with accounting personnel.

Management Override of Internal Controls

In your future audits, consider how management override of internal controls can result in faulty financial statements.

Don't allow yourself to believe that management is too honest to commit fraud. (A personal friend of mine just went to jail for stealing $3.5 million. I've known him for twenty years, so I was stunned to hear about this.) Conduct your audits to detect material misstatements, including fraud—even if you've known the management team for a long time.

Override of Controls - A Simple Summary

- Controls can be overridden in any organization
- Ways controls can be overridden include:
    - Bypassing journal entry controls to create fake journal entries
    - Using transactions outside the normal course of business —such as related party payments—to inflate earnings
    - Manipulating estimates
    - Bypassing disbursement controls so that company cash is transferred to personal bank accounts

CHAPTER 9
Okay Guys, Any Fraud Here?

Fraud can occur in any business, and yet many auditors act as though it's not an issue. The Association of Certified Fraud Examiners (ACFE) estimates that businesses lose, on average, 5% of their revenues to fraud each year. So, it's obvious: fraud is an issue. It can—and often does—lead to material misstatements in financial statements.

The Potential for Fraud

What is fraud? Well there are many definitions, but most focus on intent and deception. After all, thieves don't steal by accident, do they? Quite to the contrary, they steal on purpose and hide. A simple definition of fraud is an intentional act—usually with deception—by one or more persons to alter financial reporting or steal assets.

As auditors we consider whether one or more persons might commit fraud, resulting in material misstatements. What we don't do is make legal determinations of fraud. That's what courts do. Nevertheless, our audit risk assessment should include fraud risks if they are present.

The ACFE's biennial fraud surveys show that management fraud results in much larger losses than those committed by employees. The median fraud loss from management is usually two to three times larger than the damage from accounting personnel. So perform risk assessment with this thought in mind.

One reason auditing for fraud is so difficult is the variety of schemes. There's not just one way to steal. There's not even a dozen or a hundred ways. There are thousands of possibilities. But you can't audit for every potential fraud scheme. Still, you need an audit approach that allows you to detect material misstatements. Below I provide a framework to assess fraud risk and then respond to potential threats.

First, understand that fraudsters enrich themselves indirectly (by cooking the books) or directly (by theft).

Cooking the Books

Start your fraud risk assessment by asking, *Are there any incentives to manipulate the financial statement numbers?* For example, does the company pay bonuses based on profit? Or can management personally profit from the sale of company stock? If yes, management can steal by playing with the numbers.

Think about it: The chief financial officer can inflate profits with just one journal entry: debit receivables and credit revenue. Boom! Moreover, there are numerous other ways to increase income, such as skewing estimates or capitalizing expenses. And inflated earnings can lead to management bonuses or gains from the sale of personal stock.

Sometimes entities do, however, intentionally *understate* net income. Yes, you read that right. They understate revenues and assets or overstate expenses and liabilities. This might occur when a new management team is installed in the middle of the year, and the new team wants to make their predecessors look bad.

Cookie-jar reserves is one way to lower income. So how does this work? Management reserves income for future years. A business might, for example, increase the allowance for uncollectible receivables beyond what is reasonable. Doing so lowers income in the current year. Then, when the company is doing poorly, management reaches for the cookie jar and lowers the allowance. Magically (and fraudulently), income goes up. This is known as earnings smoothing.

The greater threat in cooking the books is an overstatement of income; but remember that some entities might desire lower income. Always consider an entity's incentives, especially those of management and those charged with governance. How would overstatements or understatements of net income or assets or liabilities benefit them?

While the median losses from theft are usually less than those from financial statement fraud, the former is more common. Why? In many smaller businesses and nonprofits, there are few incentives—such as bonuses—to manipulate the numbers. In governments, this is all the more true. So, in these types of entities, theft is the greater threat.

Theft

Employees can steal directly by taking cash, inventory, or any number of assets. Or, as we just saw, they can steal indirectly. But opportunity has to be present. And where does opportunity come from? It primarily comes through poor internal controls. Therefore, it's imperative that auditors understand the strengths and weaknesses of the internal control system.

Discovering Fraud Opportunities

There are three primary ways to understand the system of internal control and uncover fraud opportunities.

1. Walkthroughs for fraud
2. Make inquiries regarding fraud
3. Brainstorm about fraud

Walkthroughs for Fraud

We previously discussed the power of walkthroughs. As you trace a transaction through the system, you ask *what can go wrong?* One answer is theft.

As you gain an understanding of the internal controls for billing and collections, purchasing, payroll, and other transaction cycles, consider whether embezzlement can occur, and if so, how. Sometimes the potential for theft is obvious. An example of this is when one person performs all accounting duties. If an individual signs checks, reconciles bank statements, and enters the transactions, theft is possible.

In complex accounting systems (where multiple people are involved), the potential for fraud can be more difficult to discern, especially with regard to collusion. Even if accounting duties are properly segregated, collusion can enable theft. And when collusion is present, the damages can be much higher than when a lone wolf acts. Median losses are, on average, four times larger when collusion occurs, according to the ACFE's *Report to the Nations* (a fraud survey). So, as you do your walkthroughs, think about how collusion might occur.

Make Inquiries Regarding Fraud

Auditors inquire about fraud, as well as its potential. But too many auditors ask *Has fraud occurred?* and if the answer is no, they stop. We need, however, to know more than if theft occurred. We need to know if fraud opportunities are present.

This is why we ask management and employees about internal control weaknesses. They see things auditors don't, such as the controller's red Lamborghini. And if they are aware of fraud opportunities (due to control weaknesses) or red flags (such as red sports cars), we need that information.

As you make fraud inquiries, open-ended questions are your friend. You might ask, for example, *If someone desires to steal, how might they do so?* Why open-ended questions? Because closed-ended questions such as *Are you aware of any theft?* result in yes or no answers—and usually nothing else. Binary answers don't paint pictures. Open-ended questions, on the other hand, elicit richer insights. Consider using both. Typical questions might include:

- If someone wants to steal, how might they do so?
- Are you aware of or do you suspect any fraud? If yes, please describe.
- Are there any allegations or suspicions of fraud? If yes, please describe.
- How does the company prevent fraud?
- Are you aware of any violations of laws or regulations? If yes, please describe.
- How does the company ensure that violations of laws or regulations do not occur?
- Have you noticed any employee activities (red flags) that might imply potential theft? If yes, please describe.
- If you were developing a fraud prevention program for your company, what would you include?
- Are you aware of any unusual transactions during the year? If yes, please describe.
- Does the company have any related party transactions? If yes, please describe.
- How does the company ensure that financial statement disclosures are appropriate and complete?

Tailor your questions and requests based on the interviewee.

And who should you interview? Here's a list of potential persons you might inquire of:

- The accounts payable supervisor
- A receipting clerk

- The billing supervisor
- The CFO
- The CEO
- The controller
- A board member
- A sales supervisor
- A production manager

The auditing standards don't specify how many people to interview, but, at the end of the day, you want to know if fraud risks exist. I normally interview at least three persons: a board member, a key management person, and a key accounting employee. And I always interview a board member in larger organizations or an owner in smaller entities.

Notice the above list includes persons outside of accounting. Why? Because the sales supervisor can tell you a great deal about the revenue stream, whether activity is up or down, the competitive pressures, the success of the company. Likewise, a production manager can describe how inventory is created and the level of activity during the year. Inquiring of persons outside of accounting provides a broader perspective which can help you detect fraud. For example, if the CFO says sales are down 15% but the sales supervisor states they are up, you'll recognize the difference.

Some auditors send a list of fraud questions to clients to satisfy the fraud inquiry requirement. In-person fraud interviews, however, are preferable. Why? Body language says a lot in fraud interviews. Additionally, the lack of discussion will lead to a narrower understanding of fraud opportunities.

Once you've done your walkthroughs, gained an understanding of the entity and its environment, and performed your fraud inquiries, you are ready to brainstorm about potential fraud schemes.

Brainstorm About Fraud

Audit standards require that we brainstorm about how fraud might occur. The walkthrough and fraud inquiry information make brainstorming richer and more productive. So how should this process work?

First, make sure you have the right people in the conversation. That's the engagement partner (required) and other key audit team members.

Second, encourage open conversation. If you are running the meeting, ask for input—and expect it. If team members believe the engagement partner has all the answers, no one will speak. Let everyone else talk *before* the partner does.

Third, state up front, *there are no dumb ideas.* Younger staff can feel inhibited. You want them engaged, thinking, and offering insights. And as they do, include their suggestions in the team's brainstorming list.

Fourth, the engagement partner should emphasize professional skepticism. The engagement partner should encourage the team to ask the hard questions, when needed, of the client, but obviously in a professional manner.

Fifth, use a physical or electronic whiteboard to list all ideas. Most video conferencing software provides such an option.

Once the brainstorming list is complete, determine if any risks of material misstatement are present. If there are, place them on the risk assessment summary form and plan substantive procedures to address them.

Additionally, remember auditing standards require an unpredictable test each year. As you brainstorm, there is an opportunity to knock out two birds with one stone: address potential fraud and create an unpredictable test.

Next, we'll look at another risk assessment procedure: preliminary analytical procedures.

Okay Guys, Any Fraud Here? A Simple Summary

- Fraud inquiry is another risk assessment procedure and is required in all audits
- At a minimum, consider interviewing a key accounting person, a key management person, and someone from the board (or for small entities, the owner) about the occurrence of fraud or how fraud might occur
- Cooking the books is one fraud method
- Theft is another form of fraud
- Consider fraud as you perform walkthroughs
- Brainstorm with your audit team about fraud possibilities
- Note fraud possibilities or control weaknesses on the risk assessment summary form

CHAPTER 10
Preliminary Analytical Procedures

Detectives investigate crimes using tools such as fingerprints, forensic tests, interviews, timelines. Why? To bring the pieces of the puzzle together. Investigators desire to see an event, though they were not present when it occurred. Likewise, auditors use their own tools such as inquiry, observation, inspection, and analytical procedures. They desire to see a picture of the financial statements, to know whether material misstatements are present. In this chapter we will focus on another puzzle-solving aid: preliminary analytical procedures.

Preliminary Analytics

What are preliminary analytics?

Preliminary (or planning) analytics are comparisons of numbers or the use of ratios to identify potential risks of material misstatement. If revenues, for example, have been about $10 million for the last three years, but they are $15 million this year, a risk of material misstatement might be present.

So when should preliminary analytics be created?

When to Create Preliminary Analytics

Create preliminary analytics after gaining an understanding of the entity. Context provides clarity about reasonableness, and if we don't understand the entity, we may not properly assess the numbers.

Therefore, understand the entity first. Are competitive pressures present? What are the company's objectives? Are cash flow issues present? What is the normal profit margin? Does the organization have debt? By answering such questions, we develop context. And by knowing what is normal, we recognize what is abnormal.

But before creating preliminary analytics, develop expectations.

Developing Expectations

Knowing what to expect provides a basis for understanding comparative numbers and ratios. But where do expectations come from?

Here are a few sources:
- Past changes in numbers
- Discussions with management about current year operations
- Reading company minutes
- Your knowledge of events such as staffing reductions
- Non-financial statistics (e.g., the number of widgets sold)
- Your awareness of a major construction project

Information—such as that above—helps you intuit whether changes in numbers, or a lack of change, implies risk.

For example, you can expect significant sales increases or decreases; or you might anticipate little change. Regardless, document your expectations. Your workpaper could include wording such as the following:

> *Expectation: Sales have declined approximately 5% in each of the last two years. I expect sales to decline in the 3% to 5% range in the current year.*

Once you document your expectation, you are ready to create and review your preliminary analytics.

Examples of Expectations Not Met

Suppose your client's sales decreased 5% in the last two years. Would you expect a similar decrease in the current year? If yes, then an increase of 15% is a flashing light.

Or maybe you expect sales to be stable. In that case a 10% increase might be a sign of fraud.

Either situation implies a potential risk of material misstatement.

Now, let's consider the best types of planning analytics.

The Best Types of Preliminary Analytics

Auditing standards don't require particular types of planning analytics, but some, in my opinion, are better than others. Here's a suggested approach for most engagements.

First, create preliminary analytics at the financial statement reporting level. Why? Well, that's what the financial statement reader sees. So, why not use those numbers (if you can)? If financial statement level numbers are not available, use the trial balance numbers with groupers, if possible.

The purpose of preliminary analytics is to identify unexpected activity. Using detailed information (e.g., trial balance) can muddy the water. Why? There is too much information. The company might have four hundred trial balance accounts, but only fifty in the financial statements. Chasing down trial balance changes can be a waste of time, but if the financial statement numbers reveal unexpected activity, then by all means, dig deeper into trial balance comparisons.

Second, add key ratios—those tracked by management and the board—to your analytics. Many times auditors include these numbers in exit conference presentations (e.g., slide decks). If those metrics are important at the end of an audit, then they are important at the beginning.

Example ratios include:
- Inventory turnover
- Return on equity
- Days cash on hand
- Gross profit
- Debt/Equity

Other metrics, such as earnings before interest, taxes, depreciation, and amortization (EBITDA), are important for some companies. If relevant, include those in your preliminary analytics.

Hence, you create planning analytics that align with the company's focal points. And how do you know what those are? Read the entity's minutes. Most of the time you'll see the tracked ratios and numbers there.

One last thought about types of analytics: when relevant, use non-financial information, such as the number of products sold. If a company sells just three or four products and you have the sales statistics, why not compute estimates of revenues and compare them to the amounts recorded? After all, the auditing standards say that preliminary analytics may include both financial and non-financial information.

Okay, now we know about the types of analytics, but how should they be documented?

Documenting Preliminary Analytics

Here are my standard suggestions for documenting preliminary analytics.

1. Document overall expectations.
2. Include comparisons of prior-year/current-year numbers at

the financial statement level. Include multiple prior year comparisons, if possible. Include detailed revenue analytics (more about this in a moment). Include detailed analytics for other areas when warranted—for example, when financial statement level activity has unexpected changes.
3. Document key ratio comparisons when relevant.
4. Summarize your conclusions. Are there risks of material misstatement? If yes, say so. If no, say so.

Documenting Conclusions

What if there are no unexpected changes? If the numbers move (or remain stable) as you expected, no risk of material misstatement is present. **Your conclusion might read:**

Conclusion: I reviewed the changes in the account balances and noted no unexpected changes. Based on the preliminary analytics, no risks of material misstatement are noted.

Alternatively, unexpected changes might be present. You thought certain numbers would remain constant, but they moved significantly. Or you expected material changes to occur, but they did not. Again, document your conclusion. For example:

Conclusion: I expected payroll to be stable since the company's workforce remained at approximately 425 people. However, payroll expenses increased by 22%. I am placing this risk of material misstatement on the summary risk assessment work paper at 0360.

After concluding, place the identified risks on your summary risk assessment form. Later, you'll create audit steps to address those risks.

One mistake auditors make in regard to analytical documentation is commenting on every line-item variance. It's like they are attempting to explain every single change. Limit such comments to *unexpected changes*: you thought a number would increase significantly, but it did not, or you expected a number to remain constant, but a significant change is present. Once you comment on the important comparisons, then document your overall conclusion.

Now, let's consider fraud detection analytics for revenues.

Analytics for Fraudulent Revenue Recognition

Audit standards require detailed revenue analytics. Why? Because we know that companies often commit fraud by inflating revenues. Therefore, create preliminary analytics such as:

- Comparing production capacity with sales volumes
- Comparing monthly revenues and sales returns both for the period being audited and shortly thereafter

The audit standards don't require particular analytics for this purpose, but you should create comparisons that aid in your detection of fraudulent revenues. So rather than relying on analytics at the financial statement level, create a more granular analysis.

Before we close this chapter, let's address one last issue: how to create analytics for first-year businesses.

Analytics for First-Year Businesses

You may be wondering, *But what if I am auditing a new entity? How can I create analytics?* After all, new entities don't have prior period numbers.

One option is to compute expected numbers using non-financial information (e.g., the number of products manufactured or sold). Then compare the calculated numbers to the general ledger to search for unexpected variances.

A second option is to calculate ratios and compare to industry benchmarks. While industry analytics can be computed, I'm not sure how useful they are for a new company. Infant companies don't normally generate numbers comparable to mature ones. But keep this choice in your quiver—just in case.

A more useful option is the third: comparing intraperiod numbers. A monthly or quarterly trend analysis can shed light on the risk of material misstatement.

The fourth option is to review budgetary comparisons. Some entities, such as governments, lend themselves to this alternative; others (those without budgets) do not.

As you can see, there are ways to create preliminary analytics for first-year entities.

Now you see how auditors use preliminary analytical procedures to identify risks of material misstatement. Next, we will look at another part of risk assessment: reviewing the close process.

Preliminary Analytical Procedures - A Simple Summary

- Use preliminary analytics to identify unexpected activity that might reflect risks of material misstatement
- Develop expectations prior to creating preliminary analytics
- Financial statement level preliminary analytics can be used to identify unexpected activity
- Use granular preliminary analytics for revenues as a fraud detection measure
- Document expectations and conclusions for preliminary analytics
- Intraperiod analytics and budget-to-actual comparisons can be used for first-year entities
- Place any material unexpected activity on the risk assessment summary form

CHAPTER 11
The Close Process

Entities close their books at year-end and create financial statements. For small entities, this is not difficult. For larger ones, the process is more complicated. But, regardless of size, the close process is crucial to creating accurate financial statements. In risk assessment, you gain an understanding of the period-end close process.

Understanding the Close Process

The purpose of reviewing the close process is to see if there are any control weaknesses that might allow material misstatements to occur.

In smaller entities, the monthly close process can be as simple as reconciling the bank statement. A small company might wait until year-end to reconcile all balance sheet accounts, knowing that the interim financial statements aren't correct. If there are no outside parties relying on the financial statements, then a simple monthly close might be used; thereafter, the entity can clean up at year-end. Small entities might, for instance, use the cash basis of accounting during the year and convert to accrual at year-end. This works since the distribution of the monthly financial statements is usually restricted to entity personnel and the board.

Larger entities, however, usually have a rigorous monthly close process. For example, they might perform monthly procedures such as accruing all accounts payable, reconciling receivables to the general ledger, and performing periodic inventory counts. Additionally, they have team meetings to review the preliminary information, and once everything is tied down, they generate interim financial statements. These financial statements are often provided to key management personnel such as the chief executive officer or owners. Additionally, they might be provided to outside parties such as lenders.

Regardless of the entity's monthly close process, the company needs appropriate year-end financial statements. So, if the company takes shortcuts during the year, it needs to perform additional work at year-end to make sure the financial statements are complete and correct.

If the financial statements are prepared in accordance with generally accepted accounting principles, accrual-based accounting is employed. Additionally, requisite disclosures are created.

As the auditor, you want to know how your client performs their monthly and yearly closes. And, of course, you need to know how they create their financial statements. As you gain this understanding, review the related internal controls.

If the client prepares the financial statements, ask these types of questions:

- Who puts the financial statements together? What is their educational background? How much experience do they have?
- Do they use a current disclosure checklist? How are they ensuring the completeness, accuracy, and understandability of the notes?
- Does the company consolidate or combine multiple entities? If yes, what is the criteria for doing so? What is the consolidation process? Does anyone review the consolidated information before it's provided to the auditor?

- What top-side journal entries are made as the financial statements are created? Are they appropriate? Do at least two people approve the top-side entries? Are there any unusual top-side entries?
- Can you tie the financial statements to the general ledger? Is the general ledger or trial balance information placed in spreadsheets prior to creating financial statements? If yes, who has access to those spreadsheets and are changes made therein? If changes are made to the spreadsheets, who makes them and how are they documented?
- Who reviews and approves the financial statements before they are provided to the auditor?

You may be thinking *But I create the financial statements.* That is, you, the auditor, create the financial statements. That's fine, as long as a client employee oversees this nonattest service—someone with sufficient skill, knowledge, and experience. Otherwise, a self-review threat exists that impairs your independence. (Some independence rules, such as SEC, prohibit auditor preparation of financial statements. So auditors can't prepare financial statements when such rules are in play.) At the end of the day, the client has to assume responsibility for the financial statements. That means that once the auditor creates the financial statements, a client-designated person must review, approve, and assume responsibility for the financial statements. Auditors can't make management decisions, and creating financial statements is just that if there is no client review and approval process.

Obviously, if the auditor creates the financial statements, she knows how they are created. Now, the client needs to understand your process. Therefore, the auditor should provide the client with reconciliation spreadsheets, consolidation summaries, disclosure checklists, and other information used to create the financial statements. Why? So the client can review what you've done. The client needs to understand the auditor's process and details before they approve the financial statements.

Regardless of who creates the financial statements, the auditor needs to understand the process and what controls are in place to ensure the end product is materially correct. After all, one incorrect top-side journal entry can result in a material misstatement, even though the accounting system worked perfectly throughout the year.

Any significant close process control weaknesses should be noted on the risk assessment summary form.

Now let's shift gears and discuss the need to understand information technology (I.T.) controls.

The Close Process - A Simple Summary

- Material misstatements can occur in the close process as financial statements are created
- Understand the close process and related controls
- If the auditor creates the financial statements, the related documentation, such as the disclosure checklist, should be provided to the client for their review
- The client must assume responsibility for the financial statements; otherwise, the auditor is not independent
- If there are any significant close process control weaknesses, include them on the risk assessment summary form

CHAPTER 12
IT is not ET

One of my favorite movies from the 80s was *E.T. the Extra-Terrestrial*, a Steven Spielberg production. The interplay between the kids and the big-headed visitor was amusing. They didn't know what to make of each other.

Auditors can act the same way with regard to I.T. I mean what do we know about bits, clouds, and topology? These are seemingly foreign elements in a land of debits and credits. The interplay between auditors and big-headed I.T. can be interesting, but the relationship is important. Accounting systems are dependent upon sound computing environments and sound controls.

I.T.'s Impact on Risk of Material Misstatement

As you gain your understanding of I.T., remember the purpose of your work: to see if risks of material misstatement are present. If I.T. weaknesses can affect the accuracy of the financial statements, you want to know about them.

Access to Code

In many audits, we don't need a great deal of I.T. knowledge, especially if the accounting package is created by an outside party; QuickBooks is an example of this. It's less likely that someone is gaming the code for fraudulent purposes when a canned package is in use. Software coding errors are also less probable.

Larger entities, on the other hand, often write their own code for accounting components. For instance, a company might create its own inventory system that interfaces with the general ledger. Why is this important to know? Because internally created software increases the likelihood of financial statement misstatements.

Use of a Specialist

You may need the assistance of a specialist in more complicated systems. This person can come along side you and help you understand how I.T. affects accounting. In audits of smaller entities, however, the use of a specialist is usually not necessary, especially if the software is created by an outside company.

Logical Access

In understanding segregation of duties, review the logical access assignments in key transaction areas. So what is logical access? It's *who can do what*. These designations enable individuals to perform actions within the accounting software. For example, payroll personnel are given rights to the payroll module. So, as the auditor, you want to know who can perform actions such as:

- Keying in pay rates or making pay rate changes
- Adding or terminating employees
- Processing payroll
- Changing direct deposit information

As you review access assignments, see if these designations are provided on a *need to know* or *a need* to use basis. Also, see if access rights are immediately removed upon employee terminations.

Don't ask who *normally* performs accounting duties, but determine who has the *ability* to do so. Why? So you can see if appropriate segregation of duties exists. (If a person *can* change pay rates and process payments, even though he doesn't normally do so, he can steal by increasing his pay and processing direct deposits to his personal bank account.)

General Controls

Additionally, gain an understanding of general controls. These include passwords, intrusion monitoring, physical access, antivirus protection, change management, backups, recovery, and firewalls.

With the increased threat of hacking, the company should take protective measures to guard its information. For instance, someone should monitor system intrusions. But if those protections fail, the company needs recovery procedures. As the auditor, you want to know if the accounting system went down during the year, and, if it did, how the recovery went. Why? Because improper recovery can lead to material misstatements.

Spreadsheet Controls

One element often forgotten in understanding I.T. is the use of spreadsheets. Most entities use spreadsheets as a supplement to their accounting software because the accounting package doesn't provide all of the needed information. Therefore, spreadsheets act as an extension of I.T. and accounting. When in use, auditors need to know who has access to them and how they are protected. What controls ensure the soundness of the information? Are they password protected? Is spreadsheet information fed into the accounting software, or vice versa? Often key estimates, such the allowance for uncollectible accounts, are developed in spreadsheets. That's why you want to know how they are designed and if someone tests their accuracy. After all, one design flaw can lead to material error.

Outside Support and Accounting Systems

In smaller organizations, I.T. support is often outsourced. If so, you want to assess the ability of those outside persons to provide appropriate support, whether onsite or remotely.

Additionally, some components of the accounting system may reside in the cloud. If information exists offsite, you need to know if someone has vetted its security, and if so, how. Larger entities might use service organizations that are subject to audit. If service organization control (SOC) reports exist, examine them to see if there are any control weaknesses.

Once you're done reviewing I.T controls, place any significant I.T. risks on the risk assessment summary form.

You've completed part one of the book, Risk Assessment Procedures. Now it's time to learn how to use the information you've gained from your risk assessment procedures. Part two addresses how to assess the risks of material misstatement.

I.T. is Not E.T. - A Simple Summary

- I.T. control weaknesses, such as logical access issues, can lead to risks of material misstatement
- Document your understanding of I.T. and its effect on the financial statements
- Document general controls such as passwords, intrusion monitoring, physical access, antivirus protection, change management, backups, recovery, and firewalls
- Consider whether spreadsheet controls are appropriate
- Document outsourced I.T. services and cloud-based accounting components; review service organization reports (SOC reports) when services may lead to risks of material misstatement
- Consider whether you need the assistance of an I.T. specialist
- Place any material I.T. risks on the risk assessment summary form

PART TWO
Assessing the Risks of Material Misstatement

CHAPTER 13
The Audit Risk Model

When you pour the pieces of a puzzle onto a table, they lie there without meaning. But as you put them together, they create a picture. I like to start with the edge pieces and work my way inward. The edge is easier; the inner parts, more difficult.

Risk Assessment Puzzle

The same is true of the risk assessment puzzle. Some parts—such as client acceptance, computing materiality, reviewing the close process—are easy. Others—such as understanding activity-level controls and the potential for fraud—tend to be challenging. Regardless, all of the pieces are necessary to see the whole.

Now it's time to put the puzzle together. After all, we've already worked through the following:

- Client acceptance or continuance
- Computing materiality and performance materiality
- Gaining an understanding of the entity and its environment
- Understanding the entity-level controls
- Understanding the activity-level controls
- Performing walkthroughs
- Considering the possibility of management override
- Looking for fraud opportunities and related control weaknesses
- Creating preliminary analytics

- Reviewing the close process
- Examining the information technology system

We now have the disparate pieces that make up the whole. And as we place the risks of material misstatement side-by-side, we will see the risk assessment picture take shape. There's the outline, the color, the substance. Yes, we can see it clearly now.

And once the picture is complete, we know what needs attention. If, for example, a payables fraud is possible, we'll develop substantive procedures to lessen that risk of material misstatement. If inventory has control weaknesses, we'll create procedures to lower those risks. If we have questions about management's integrity, we'll respond by using more experienced staff.

The risk picture is the basis for our audit plan. If there are few risks, then our responses will be few. But if there are several threats, more work is necessary. This is the beauty of risk assessment: done correctly, it tells us what is necessary and what is not. Risk assessment creates both effectiveness and efficiency.

With the risk picture we can plan our further audit procedures using the audit risk model.

Audit Risk Model

So what is audit risk?

It's the risk of expressing an inappropriate audit opinion when material misstatements are present. For example, issuing an unmodified opinion when material misstatements exist is audit failure. Obviously, this is not desirable. So, let's see how we can leverage the audit risk model to ensure a correct opinion.

The audit risk model is defined as follows:

Audit risk = Inherent risk **x** *Control risk* **x** *Detection risk*

Think of these risks in this manner:

Inherent risk - the chance an account balance, a transaction class, or a disclosure will have a material misstatement due to its nature (risky or not risky) without regard for controls

Control risk - the chance that the entity's internal controls will not prevent or detect material misstatements in a timely manner

Detection risk - the chance that the auditor will not detect material misstatements

The first two (inherent risk and control risk) live in the company's accounting system. The third (detection risk) lies with the audit firm.

The risk of material misstatements is defined this way:

Risk of material misstatement = Inherent risk **x** *Control risk*

As the risk of material misstatement (the company's risk) increases, the auditor's work increases. Put another way: as the client's risk increases, the auditor performs more work. Why? So she can lower her detection risk.

To understand the audit risk model, consider the following tale of a villain.

A Tale of a Villain

A villain (inherently a thief) desires to make his way into your home. You have locks on your doors and an alarm system (controls, if you will). But you forget to lock your back door and the alarm is not set. During the night, the thief comes in and steals money and other possessions. So, you call the police (the detectives). Why? To see if everything is okay and to help determine what was stolen.

This is the audit risk model in physical form.

A risky transaction is a villain. Its nature is to be wrong (inherent risk). If internal controls are weak or absent (control risk), misstatement occurs. And if the auditor fails to detect the misstatement (detection risk), the villain's damage goes unnoticed.

In audits, the villain and his damages can exist without notice. Material misstatements develop and survive because they are hidden. And a misstatement, if material, can lead to audit failure.

But how do misstatements hide? Sometimes a client commits fraud and intentionally shrouds the deception. Other times mistakes are made, but the volume of transactions hides the misstatement. Either way, undetected misstatements can be a significant problem.

Your ability to create a sound audit plan comes from properly understanding and assessing inherent risk and control risk. So, we're going to unpack both of these. But, before we do, let's consider relevant assertions.

The Audit Risk Model - A Simple Summary

- Audit risk = Inherent risk x Control risk x Detection risk
- Risk of material misstatement = Inherent risk x Control risk
- Your ability to create a sound audit plan comes from properly understanding and assessing inherent risk and control risk
- As the risk of material misstatement increases, the auditor increases further audit procedures to lower detection risk

CHAPTER 14
Relevant Assertions

All businesses make assertions in their financial statements. For example, when a financial statement has a cash balance of $605,432, the business asserts that the cash *exists*. When the allowance for uncollectibles is $234,100, the entity asserts that the amount is properly *valued*. And when payables are shown at $58,980, the company asserts that the liability is *complete*.

Reporting Framework

Of course assertions derive their meaning from the reporting framework. So before you consider assertions, make sure you know what the reporting framework is and the requirements therein. For example, the occurrence of $4 million in revenue means one thing under GAAP and quite another when using the cash basis of accounting.

Relevant Assertions

For an auditor, relevant assertions are those where a risk of material misstatement is reasonably possible. So, magnitude (is the risk related to a material amount?) and likelihood (is it reasonably possible?) are both considered.

Maybe you believe cash could be stolen, so you are concerned about *existence*. Is the cash really there? Or with payables, you know the client has historically not recorded all invoices, so the recorded amount might not be *complete*. And the pension disclosure is so complicated that you believe it may not be *accurate*. If you believe the risk of material misstatement is reasonably possible for these areas, then the assertions are relevant.

Assertions

Assertions include:

- Existence or occurrence (E/O)
- Completeness (C)
- Accuracy, valuation, or allocation (A/V)
- Rights and obligations (R/O)
- Presentation, disclosure, and understandability (P/D)
- Cutoff (CU)

Not all auditors use the same assertions. In other words, they might use assertions different from those listed above, or the auditor could list each assertion separately. Regardless, auditors need to make sure they address all possible areas of misstatement.

Assessing Risk at the Assertion Level

Think of assertions as a scoping tool that allows you to focus on the essential. Not all assertions are relevant to account balances, transaction cycles, or disclosures. Usually, one or more assertions are relevant to an account balance, but not all. For example, existence, rights, and cutoff might be relevant to cash, but not valuation (provided there is no foreign currency) or understandability (there's nothing complicated about cash). A reasonable possibility of material misstatement is usually not present for valuation or understandability.

As you consider the significant account balances, transaction areas, and disclosures, specify the relevant assertions and assess risk at that level. Why? So you can determine the risk of material misstatement for each and create responses.

Accounts Payable and Expense Assertions Example

Here's an example for accounts payable and expenses.

	ASSERTION	INHERENT RISK	CONTROL RISK	RMM	RESPONSE
Area of Accounts Payable/Expenses	E/O	Moderate	High	Moderate	Perform substantive analytics comparing expenses to budget and prior year
	C	High	High	High	Perform search for unrecorded liabilities
	CU	Low	High	Moderate	Substantive analytical comparison of the payable balance

INHERENT RISK SUPPORT

Accounts payable is not complex and there are no new accounting standards related to it. There are no subjective judgments. Volume is moderate and directional risk is an understatement. Inherent risk is assessed at high for completeness (client has not fully recorded payables in prior years). Occurrence and cutoff have not been a problem areas in past years.

Risk of material misstatement is the result of inherent risk and control risk. Auditors often assess control risk at high because they don't plan to test for control effectiveness—more about that in the Control Risk chapter. If control risk is assessed at high, then inherent risk becomes the driver of the risk of material misstatement. In the table above, the auditor believes there is a reasonable possibility that a material misstatement might occur for occurrence, completeness, and cutoff. Thus responses are planned for each.

Accounts Payable and Expense Assertions Example with a Significant Risk

Fraud risks and subjective estimates can be (and usually are) assessed at the upper end of the spectrum of inherent risk. They are, therefore, significant risks. When a significant risk is present, the auditor should perform procedures beyond his or her normal approach. As we previously said, when the client's risk increases, the level of testing increases. The payables/expenses assessment below incorporates an additional response due to a significant risk: the risk that fictitious vendors might exist.

Area of Accounts Payable/Expenses

ASSERTION	INHERENT RISK	CONTROL RISK	RMM	RESPONSE
E/O	High	High	High	Perform substantive analytics comparing expenses to budget and prior year; Perform fictitious vendor test
C	High	High	High	Perform search for unrecorded liabilities
CU	Low	High	Moderate	Substantive analytical comparison of the payable balance

INHERENT RISK SUPPORT

Accounts payable is not complex and there are no new accounting standards related to it. There are no subjective judgments. The company suffered a fictitious vendor fraud during the year, so the occurrence assertion has uncertainty. Volume is moderate and directional risk is an understatement. Inherent risk is assessed at high for occurrence (significant risk) and completeness. Cutoff has not been a problem in past years.

In auditing expenses, the auditor knows that there is a risk that fictitious vendors exist. In this scheme, the payables clerk adds and makes payments to nonexistent vendors. Additionally, the payments are usually supported with fake invoices. What is the result? Additional expenses. Those fraudulent payments appear as expenses in the income statement. So the occurrence assertion is suspect.

If the auditor believes the risk of fictitious vendors is at the upper end of the inherent risk spectrum, then a significant risk is present in relation to the occurrence assertion. And such a risk deserves a fraud detection procedure. In this example, the auditor responds by adding a substantive test for detection of fictitious vendors. More risk, more work.

Additionally, notice the inherent risk for occurrence is assessed at high. Why? Because it's at the upper end of the *inherent* risk spectrum. A significant risk is, by definition, a high inherent risk, never low or moderate.

As you can tell, I am suggesting that risk be assessed at the assertion level. But let's see if it's ever acceptable to assess risk at the transaction level.

Assessing Risk at the Transaction Level

Is it okay do the following?

AREA	ASSERTION	INHERENT RISK	CONTROL RISK	RMM
Cash	E/O; CU; R/O; A/V; P/D	High	High	High

The inherent risk assessment for all assertions in an account balance are seldom the same. So it is not advisable to assess risk in the manner shown above. Also, assessing risk at the transaction level could result in a peer review finding.

Those who assess risk at the account or transaction level think they are saving time. But is this a more efficient approach? Or might it be more economical to assess risk at the assertion level?

Assess Risk at the Assertion Level

If the goal of assessing risk is to quickly complete a risk assessment document (and nothing else), then assessing risk at the transaction level makes sense. But the purpose of risk assessment is to provide planning direction. Therefore, we need to assess risk at the assertion level.

Why? Let's answer that question with an accounts payable example.

Suppose the auditor assesses risk at the transaction level, assessing all accounts payable assertions at high. What does this mean? It means the auditor should perform substantive procedures to respond to the high-risk assessments for each assertion. Why? The risk assessment for valuation, existence, rights and obligations, completeness, and all other assertions are high. Logically, the substantive procedures must now address all of these high risks.

Alternatively, what if the accounts payable completeness assertion is assessed at high and all other assertions are at low to moderate? How does this impact the audit plan? Now the auditor plans and performs a search for unrecorded liabilities. Additionally, he may not, for example, perform existence-related procedures such as sending vendor confirmations. The lower risk assertions require less work.

Do you see the advantage of assessing risk at the assertion level? Rather than using an inefficient approach—let's audit everything—the auditor pinpoints audit procedures based on risk.

And what are the benefits of assessing risk at the assertion level?

- Efficient work
- Higher profits
- Conformity with standards

Your Audit Files

Look at two or three of your audit files and review your risk assessments. Are you assessing risk at the transaction level or at the assertion level? If at the assertion level, you're good. If at the transaction level, then in the future, plan to assess risk at the assertion level. That way you can properly document risks and avoid one of those nasty peer review comments.

Next, we'll look at inherent risk.

Relevant Assertions - A Simple Summary

- All entities make assertions such as cash *exists*
- Relevant assertions are those where a risk of material misstatement is reasonably possible

- All assertions are usually not relevant for an account balance, a transaction cycle, or for a disclosure
- Fraud risks and subjective estimate risks assessed at the upper end of the spectrum of inherent risk are significant risks
- Significant risks require an appropriate response in the form of a test of details (a further audit procedure)
- Risks of material misstatement should be assessed at the assertion level

CHAPTER 15
Inherent Risk

What is inherent risk? It is the chance an account balance, a transaction class, or a disclosure will possess a material misstatement due to its nature (risky or not risky) without regard for controls.

Inherent Risk Factors

Examples of factors to consider in assessing inherent risk include the following:

- Susceptibility to theft or fraudulent reporting
- Complex accounting or calculations
- Need for subjective judgment
- Difficulty in creating disclosures
- Size and volume of accounts balance or transactions
- Susceptibility to obsolescence
- Uncertainty about a balance, disclosure, classification

Inherent risk is not an average of these factors. Just one risk can make an account balance, transaction cycle, or disclosure high risk. Nevertheless, auditors should consider all relevant influences. If anything increases the risk of misstatement—again, without regard for controls—then it's an inherent risk factor.

Here are examples of inherent risk factors and their effect on assertions:

CIRCUMSTANCE	RISK FACTORS	ASSERTIONS
High-tech inventory is becoming obsolete	Obsolescence	Valuation
A nonprofit receives a great deal of cash	Susceptible to theft	Existence/occurrence
A healthcare company has a defined benefit plan with complex pension plan disclosures	Complexity; difficulty in creating the disclosure	Presentation, disclosure, and understandability
A manufacturing business has several stages of inventory development	Complexity	Accuracy and allocation
A bank's allowance for loan loss computation is complex	Complexity	Valuation
A company loan has debt covenants and the entity has financial problems	Uncertainty	Presentation, disclosure, and understandability
Company has convertible debt; instrument is highly complex	Complexity	Presentation, disclosure, and understandability
A landfill just opened near the corporate office; possible asset impairment	Subjective judgment	Valuation
Company purchases land in a foreign country as an investment; land prices are volatile	Subjective judgment	Valuation
Accounts payable accrual was understated for the last four years	Fraudulent reporting	Completeness
Entity has ongoing losses and deficits in equity; potential going concern disclosures	Uncertainty; subjective judgment; difficulty in creating the disclosure	Presentation, disclosure, and understandability

In assessing inherent risks, auditors should also consider directional risk.

Directional Risk

When an entity desires to make itself look better than it really is, it can inflate assets and revenues or decrease liabilities and expenses. It might also intentionally leave out required disclosures. These tendencies are referred to as directional risk, and they can affect inherent risk.

In considering directional risk, ask yourself questions such as:

- Who will use the financial statements?
- Are the owners preparing to sell the company or a division?
- Were there any consistent understatements or overstatements of accounts in prior periods?
- Are there any debt covenants requiring particular ratios or profitability levels?
- Are management bonuses dependent upon profits?
- Does the company need gains or losses to take advantage of tax positions?

Allow these considerations to inform your inherent risk assessments. Your client may be honest and might not play with the numbers, but our job as auditors is to exercise professional skepticism. Considerations such as those listed above can drive inherent risk upward.

Some account balances and disclosures, however, are not risky.

Inherent Risk at Less Than High

When inherent risk is less than high, you can perform fewer or less rigorous further audit procedures.

An example of a low inherent risk is the existence assertion for payables. The directional risk of payables is usually an understatement, not an overstatement. Therefore, the lower risk assessment for existence allows the auditor to perform less work in relation to this assertion.

Conversely, the completeness assertion for accounts payable is commonly assessed at high for inherent risk. Businesses can inflate their profits by accruing fewer payables. That's why auditors perform a search for unrecorded liabilities.

Base your risk assessment on factors such as those listed above. If inherent risk is legitimately low, then great. You can perform fewer further audit procedures. But if the inherent risk is high, assess it accordingly—even if that means more work. Peer reviewers look for support (the basis) for inherent risk assessments, and these should be documented. So describe the rationale for your assessments.

Auditors can (though they should not) intentionally assess inherent risk at levels lower than what is merited.

Improper Inherent Risk Assessments

Auditors can manipulate inherent risk in order to perform less work. Obviously, this is not appropriate, but it's a possibility. Auditors want to make a profit on their engagements, so they could cut corners by assessing inherent risk at levels lower than what is warranted. The lower inherent risk results in a lower risk of material misstatement, which leads to less work.

Additionally, auditors can make mistakes in assessing inherent risk. These errors occur when the auditor doesn't recognize a relevant assertion: a material misstatement is reasonably possible for an assertion, but the auditor doesn't realize it. So the risk is not assessed for the assertion. Errors also happen when the auditor mistakenly assesses inherent risk at low or moderate, but it should be higher.

So, we see that auditors can intentionally or by mistake understate inherent risk assessments. Therefore, audit file reviewers should take a look at the inherent risk assessments to see if they are appropriate.

Now, let's consider another potential: inherent risks are assessed too high.

Proper Inherent Risk Assessments

Assessing inherent risk too high can result in an opposite effect: too much audit work. Risk assessments that are too low can result in higher detection risk. That is, the auditor may not respond with an appropriate level of work. But auditors can assess inherent risk too high and over-audit.

Suppose an auditor assesses a risk as significant, believing the inherent risk is at the higher end of the spectrum of inherent risk. But the risk is actually moderate. The significant risk assessment triggers further audit procedures and wasted effort. The auditor is responding to a risk that is not present, or at least responding at a level not merited. It's money down the drain.

Of course peer reviewers are less likely to ding you for performing too much work, but your engagement profits will suffer.

So we need to assess inherent risk at the right level: not too low and not too high. (Reminds me of Goldilocks and the three bears.)

Significant Risks

Significant risks are those in the upper end of the spectrum of inherent risk. For example, a construction contractor's estimate of costs to complete contracts is often a significant risk. Another example of a significant risk is a nonprofit that receives large amounts of cash contributions. So complex estimates and potential theft areas can be significant risks. Auditors must use a test of details in regard to significant risk areas. Therefore, if an auditor identifies a significant risk in her risk assessment summary form, she should plan a test of details to address it. (See the Test of Details chapter to learn more.)

Now that you know how to assess inherent risk, let's shift our gaze to control risk.

Inherent Risk - A Simple Summary
- Inherent risk is the chance an account balance, a transaction class, or a disclosure will possess a material misstatement due to its nature (risky or not risky) without regard for controls
- Inherent risk is affected by factors such as complexity, subjectivity, and uncertainty
- Directional risk—the bias that management has for an overstatement or understatement of a number—affects inherent risk
- Assessing inherent risk appropriately is a key to determining further audit procedures
- Significant risks are those in the upper end of the spectrum of inherent risk

CHAPTER 16
Control Risk

What is control risk? It's the chance that an entity's internal controls will not prevent or detect material misstatements in a timely manner.

Companies develop internal controls to manage inherent risk. The greater the inherent risk, the greater the need for controls.

Audit Risk Model

As we begin this chapter, think about control risk in the context of the audit risk model:

Audit risk = Inherent risk **x** *Control risk* **x** *Detection risk*

Recall the client's risk is made up of inherent risk and control risk. And the remainder, detection risk, is what the auditor controls. Auditors gain an understanding of inherent risk and control risk. Why? To develop their audit plan and lower their detection risk (the risk that the audit will not detect material misstatements). Put more simply, the auditor understands the client's risk in order to lower her own risk.

Further Audit Procedures

How does the auditor reduce detection risk? With further audit procedures. Those include test of controls and substantive procedures (test of details or substantive analytics). We'll examine these in coming chapters.

After the auditor gains an understanding of the entity and its environment, including internal controls, control risk is often assessed at high. Why? Two reasons: one has to do with efficiency and the other with weak internal controls.

Assessing Control Risk at High

Consider the first reason for high control risk assessments: efficiency.

Control risk can be assessed at high, even if you see that controls are properly designed and in use during your walkthroughs. But why would you assess control risk at high when controls are okay?

Let me answer that question with a billing and collection example.

You can test billing and collection internal controls for effectiveness (assuming your walkthrough reveals appropriate controls). But if this test takes eight hours and a substantive approach takes five hours, which is more efficient? Obviously, the substantive approach. And if you use a fully substantive approach, you must assess control risk at high for all relevant assertions.

At this point, you may still be thinking, *But, Charles, if controls are appropriately designed and implemented, why is control risk high?* Because a test of controls is required for control risk assessments below high: the auditor needs a basis (evidence) for the lower assessment. And a walkthrough is not (in most cases) considered a test of controls for effectiveness; it does not provide a sufficient basis for the lower risk assessment. A walkthrough provides an initial impression about controls, but that impression can be wrong. That's why a test of controls is necessary when control risk is below high; the test proves the effectiveness of the control.

In our example above, a substantive approach is more efficient than testing controls. So we plan a substantive approach and assess control risk at high for all relevant assertions.

Now, let's look at the second reason for high control risk assessments: weak internal controls. Here again, allow me to explain why control risk should be high by way of example.

If the billing and collection cycle walkthrough reveals weak internal controls, then control risk is high. Why? Because the controls are not designed appropriately or they are not in use. In other words, they would not prevent or detect a material misstatement. You *could* test those controls for effectiveness. But why would you? They are ineffective. Consequently, control risk has to be high. Why? Again, because there is no basis for the lower control risk assessment. Even if you tested controls, the result would not support a lower control risk assessment: the controls are not working.

If, on the other hand, controls are appropriate, then you might test them (though you are not required to).

Assessing Control Risk at Less than High

What if, based on your walkthrough, controls are okay? Furthermore, what if you believe the test of controls will take four hours while a substantive approach will take eight hours? Then you can test controls for effectiveness. And if the controls are effective, you can assess control risk at less than high. Now you have support for the lower control risk assessment.

But what if you test controls for effectiveness and the controls are not working? Then a substantive approach is your only choice.

Many auditors don't test controls for this reason: they are afraid the test of controls will prove the controls are ineffective. For example, if you test sixty transactions for the issuance of a purchase order, and seven transactions are without purchase orders, the sample does not support effectiveness. The result is that the test of controls is a waste of time.

Some auditors mistakenly believe they don't need an understanding of controls because they plan to use a fully substantive audit approach. But is this true?

Fully Substantive Audit Approach

Weak internal controls can result in more substantive procedures, even if you normally use a substantive approach.

Suppose you assess control risk at high for all billing and collection cycle assertions and plan to use a fully substantive approach. Now, consider two scenarios: one where the entity has weak controls, and another where controls are strong.

Billing and Collection Cycle - Weak Controls

Think about a business that has a cash receipt process with few internal controls. **Suppose the following is true:**

- Two employees receipt cash
- They both work from one cash drawer
- The two employees provide receipts to customers, but only if requested
- They apply the payments to the customer's accounts, but they also have the ability to adjust (reduce or write off) customer balances
- At the end of the day, one of the two employees creates a deposit slip and deposits the money at a local bank (though this is not always done in a timely manner)
- These same employees also create and send bills to customers
- Additionally, they reconcile the related bank account

Obviously, a segregation of duties problem exists and theft could occur. For example, the clerks could steal money and write off the related receivables. Child's play.

Billing and Collection Cycle - Strong Controls

But suppose the owner detects theft and fires the two employees. He does background checks on the replacements. **Now the following is true:**

- A separate cash drawer is assigned to each clerk
- The controller is required to review customer account adjustments on a daily basis (the controller can't adjust receivable accounts)
- The cash receipt clerks reconcile their daily activity to a customer receipts report, and the money along with the report is provided to the controller
- The controller counts the daily funds received and reconciles the money to the cash receipts report
- Then the controller creates a deposit slip and provides the funds and deposit slip to a courier
- Once the deposit is made, the courier gives the bank deposit receipt to the controller
- A fourth person (that does not handle cash) reconciles the bank statement in a timely manner
- The monthly customer bills are created and mailed by someone not involved in the receipting process
- Moreover, the owner reviews a monthly cash receipts report

Now, let me ask you: would you use the same substantive audit procedures for each of the above scenarios? Hopefully not. The first situation begs for a fraud test. For example, we might test the adjustments to receivables on a sample basis. Why? To ensure the clerks are not writing off customer balances and stealing cash.

Audit Procedures: Basic and Extended

Basic audit procedures for the billing and collection cycle might include:

- Test the period-end bank reconciliation
- Create substantive analytics for receivable balances and revenues
- Confirm receivable accounts and examine subsequent receipts

We perform these basic procedures whether controls are strong or weak. But we would add extended substantive procedures, such as testing accounts receivable adjustments, when controls are weak and might allow theft.

Do you see how the understanding of controls impacts planning (even when control risk is assessed at high)? If we were unaware of the control weaknesses, we would not plan the needed fraud detection procedures.

In summary, we need to understand controls even if we plan to use a fully substantive approach, and even if control risks are assessed at high for all assertions. More risk means more audit work.

Now that we've covered inherent risk and control risk, let's use these to determine the risk of material misstatement, which is the topic of our next chapter.

Control Risk - A Simple Summary

- Control risk is the probability that an entity's internal controls will not prevent or detect material misstatements in a timely manner
- Internal control weaknesses may require a control risk assessment of high
- Control risk can only be assessed below high when a test of control proves the control to be effective (the test of control provides the basis for the lower control risk assessment)

- If walkthroughs show controls to be appropriately designed and implemented, the auditor can (1) assess control risk at high and use a fully substantive approach, or (2) assess control risk below high and test controls for effectiveness, whichever is most efficient
- Even if an auditor intends to use a fully substantive approach, walkthroughs are necessary to determine if additional substantive tests are needed; additional substantive procedures may be necessary when material fraud is possible due to internal control weaknesses

CHAPTER 17
Risks of Material Misstatement

Using inherent risk and control risk, we determine the risks of material misstatement for each relevant assertion. Then we create further audit procedures to respond to the identified risks. Moreover, we link the risks to the responses (further audit procedures).

Some risks, however, are not amenable to risk assessment at the assertion level. Those occur at the financial statement level and call for a broader response, such as assigning more experienced audit staff.

Below you'll see guidance about assessing risk at the assertion level and then at the financial statement level.

Assessing Risks at the Assertion Level

When inherent risk and control risk are the same, the resulting risk of material misstatement is easy to determine. For example, if inherent risk is high and control risk is high, then the risk of material misstatement is high. But what if the two are different?

Suppose your inherent risk is moderate and your control risk is high. What is the risk of material misstatement? Moderate or high? It depends.

Audit standards don't tell us to use *low*, *moderate*, and *high* in assessing risk. Nevertheless, use of these levels is a common audit practice. You could, alternatively, use a scale of 1 to 5. If you did, computing the risk of material misstatement might be easier. But if you use low, moderate, and high, then the resulting risk of material misstatement is based on your judgment regarding inherent risk and control risk. Here's an example using plant, property, and equipment.

Plant, Property, and Equipment Example

The inherent risk for a building's existence assertion is low. In most cases, a building is purchased and placed on the books. Thereafter, the asset is depreciated over its economic life. There's nothing complicated about this, and there's no risk of theft. If you assess control risk at high, what is your risk of material misstatement? I'd say low. Even if no controls exist, it's very unlikely the accounting for the building will be incorrect.

So, in this example, a low inherent risk and a high control risk yields a low risk of material misstatement. As a result, my audit response will be minimal. If property, plant, and equipment is material as a whole, then I must perform substantive procedures since the audit standards require that I do so. Therefore, I would probably use substantive analytics, a comparison of this year's numbers with the prior year.

But suppose an earthquake occurs near the building and it is damaged. Now the valuation assertion comes into play, and I might assess the inherent risk at moderate (or high) depending on the amount of damage. If control risk is high for valuation, what is your risk of material misstatement? It depends on your judgment. If material damage occurred, then the risk of material misstatement is probably high. And what would the further audit procedure be? A review of a real estate appraisal created by a licensed appraiser.

Responses to Risks of Material Misstatement

Your responses to risks of material misstatement can be as follows:

RISKS OF MATERIAL MISSTATEMENT	RESPONSE
Low	No audit program
Moderate	Audit program; basic procedures
High	Audit program; basic and extended procedures

So if all assertions for prepaid assets, for example, are low and the amount is not material, then no audit program is necessary.

The responses are the further audit procedures which include (1) test of details, (2) substantive analytics, and (3) test of controls. (See part three of this book, Responses to Risks of Material Misstatement, for information about further audit procedures.) We use further audit procedures to create our audit plan which is comprised of audit programs. Audit programs are created for account balance or transaction cycles such as cash, receivables and revenues, inventory, payables and expenses, debt, and equity. Each audit program consists of particular procedures such as sending bank confirmations or counting inventory.

Linkage

Sometimes firms say to me, *I know I over-audit, but I don't know how to lessen my work.* And then they say, *How can I reduce my time without reducing quality?*

Here's my answer: Perform real risk assessments and document the risks of material misstatement at the assertion level. Then tailor—yes, change the audit program—to address the risks. Next, perform further audit procedures related to the identified risk areas—and slap yourself every time you even think about *same as last year.*

Once you've assessed the risks of material misstatement, link your risk assessment to your responses (audit procedures). This can be done on the risk assessment summary form. For example, you might state what the responses are. Those responses can be in a column next to the risks of material misstatement, or you could add them below your risk assessment table. (See the example risk assessment tables in the Relevant Assertions chapter.) I primarily include my responses for salient risks on the risk assessment form. I am not, however, including my entire audit program on the form. Additionally, in the audit programs, note the assertions being addressed next to each audit procedure.

The main point of linkage is to show how particular audit steps address specific risks. If canned audit programs are used with no regard for risk, then the audit steps may not be responsive—and the risk assessment process has no value. We need to tailor the audit program and link the audit steps to our risk assessment. In other words, risk assessment drives the selection of audit procedures.

Assessing Risk at the Financial Statement Level

As we've already said, it's desirable to assess risk at the assertion level; but some risks are broad, such as whether the financial statements should include a variable interest entity. The inclusion or exclusion of another entity can affect many accounts and disclosures.

Also, some risks are not amenable to risk assessment at the assertion level. For example, management override is pervasive and affects many accounts and many assertions. Another example is the hiring of a new chief financial officer. Since you've never worked with him before, you're not sure if he is competent. These broader risks can be responded to with broader responses, such as appointing more experienced audit staff or providing more supervision. Financial statement level risks and responses should be documented, usually on your risk assessment summary form.

Now you know how to assess the risks of material misstatement. In the coming chapters I'll tell you how to plan your audit.

Risks of Material Misstatements - A Simple Summary

- The risk of material misstatement is comprised of inherent risk and control risk
- Auditors should assess risk at the assertion level and at the financial statement level
- Financial statement level risks are broad and require general responses such as assigning experienced staff to the audit
- Assertion level risk can be assessed at low, moderate, or high
- Auditors plan their responses to risks of material misstatement by creating audit programs that are comprised of further audit procedures
- Link your risks of material misstatement to your planned responses

PART THREE
Responses to Risks of Material Misstatement

CHAPTER 18
Audit Strategy and Plan

Before NASA put a man on the moon, they had a strategy. It could have read as follows:

> *We will put a man on the moon. The significant factors of our mission include mathematical computations, gravitational pull, thrust, and mechanics. The risks include the loss of our astronauts' lives, so we need to provide sufficient food, air, sound communications, and a safe vessel. The deliverable will be the placement of one man on the moon and the safe return of our three astronauts. The engagement team will include three astronauts, launch personnel at Kennedy Space Center, and mission-control employees in Houston, Texas.*

A sound strategy led to Neil Armstrong's historic walk on July 20, 1969.

Our audit strategy—in a more pedestrian pursuit—is a summary of objectives, resources, and risk. It's the big picture. Our strategy leads to the successful issuance of our audit opinion (not quite as exciting as walking on the moon, but hey, it's still important).

What's in an Audit Strategy?

The audit strategy doesn't have to be complicated or long, especially for smaller entities—it can be a short memo. So what are we after? A summary of risks, needed resources, and objectives.

What's in the audit strategy?

- Characteristics of the engagement
- Reporting objectives
- Significant factors
- Results of preliminary engagement activities
- Knowledge gained from other similar engagements
- Resources and when they will be needed

We are documenting:

- The scope
- The objectives (e.g., GAAS opinion, Yellow Book report, Single Audit)
- The significant factors (e.g., Is this a new or complex entity?)
- The risk assessment (e.g., high risk areas)
- The planned resources (e.g., the engagement team)

If your forms provider does not give you a strategy form, consider creating one. **Here are some areas that can be addressed:**

- Deliverables and deadlines
- A time budget
- The audit team, including any specialists
- Key client contacts and their experience
- New accounting standards affecting the audit
- Problems encountered in the prior year
- Anticipated challenges in the current year
- Partner directions regarding key risk areas

Audit Strategy as the Central Document

If there is any one document that summarizes the entire audit, this is it. As you can see, the strategy is general in nature, so you also need a detailed plan to satisfy the demands of the strategy—this is the audit plan (commonly referred to as audit programs).

NASA had a mission statement for Apollo 11, but also had written guidelines to direct the step-by-step execution of the project.

Audit Plan

Along with the audit strategy, the auditor creates an audit plan (made up of audit programs by transaction areas) to respond to risks. Technically, the audit plan encompasses risk assessment procedures, but we are presently addressing responses to identified risk. Audit programs spell out the nature, timing, and extent of procedures to be performed. Additionally, these further audit procedures are linked to assertions in account balances, transaction cycles, and disclosures.

Further audit procedures include:

1. Test of details
2. Substantive analytics
3. Test of controls

The first two—test of details and substantive analytics—comprise the available substantive procedures. And the third—test of controls—is the remaining option. Once auditors assess the risks of material misstatements, they plan their further audit procedures. For instance, an auditor vouches additions to plant, property, and equipment to invoices (a test of details). Why? She believes capitalized amounts might be overstated. In other words, she is addressing the existence assertion. Therefore, an audit step in the plant, property, and equipment audit program could be added such as: *Vouch significant plant, property, and equipment additions to supporting documentation including invoices.*

Required Further Audit Procedures

Of the three further audit procedures, are certain ones required? Yes.

First, a test of controls is necessary if substantive procedures alone can't provide sufficient audit evidence at the assertion level. For example, when a benefit plan participant goes online to change his 401(k) investment options, there may be no physical documents to examine (in a benefit plan audit). Therefore, a test of controls might be the only option.

Second, a test of details is necessary when significant risks are present. So if, for example, a complex estimate is present, a test of details is required. Likewise, if a fraud risk is present, a test of details is required.

Third, substantive procedures are required for each material class of transactions, account balances, and disclosures—even if the risk of material misstatement is low. If debt, for example, is material and the risk of material misstatement is low, use a substantive procedure to address the relevant assertions in this balance. Why? Because there's a chance that the risk assessment is not correct. Moreover, management override of controls is always possible.

Another reason to test low risk areas is the possibility of a black swan.

Black Swans in Audits

Nassim Nicholas Taleb wrote a book titled *The Black Swan, The Impact of the Highly Improbable.* In it he describes how improbable events lead to devastating effects. Think about COVID-19: highly improbable, but the effects were catastrophic.

In audits, you need to consider if a black swan is present, even if you don't believe an assertion is relevant because the risk of material misstatement is low. High impact, low probability events do occur. So after you've done your risk assessments, step back and examine all possibilities. Is there a niggling possibility that needs to be addressed? Then address it, not because it's reasonably possible, but because the effects—if they occur—could create significant problems.

Now let's move from the audit strategy to the audit plan which includes the use of further audit procedures.

First up: test of details.

Audit Strategy and Plan - A Simple Summary
- Create an audit strategy comprised of information such as reporting objectives, resources needed, deliverables and deadlines, anticipated challenges, and key risk areas
- Document your audit plan by creating audit programs
- Audit programs contain the following further audit procedures:
    - Test of details
    - Substantive analytics
    - Test of controls
- Consider whether low probability, high impact risks are present and plan responses if needed

CHAPTER 19
Test of Details

Audit standards don't define tests of details. They only say that a test of details is one of two substantive procedure options (the other being substantive analytics).

Examples of Test of Details

Since there is no definition, here are a few examples of test of details:

- Vouching payable invoices
- Tracing bills sent to customers
- Search for unrecorded liabilities in accounts payable
- Testing bank reconciliations by examining subsequent month bank statements
- Sending bank confirmations
- Sending customer confirmations
- Agreeing receivables to contracts
- Vouching subsequent receipts in receivables
- Reconciling payroll in the general ledger to quarterly payroll tax returns

As you can see, a *test of details* is just what the term says: auditing transaction details. By contrast, auditors use *substantive analytics* to look at numbers from a broader perspective. For example, the auditor might compute the current ratio or compare this year's debt level with prior years. (See the next chapter for Substantive Analytics.)

Significant Risks

Recall from the inherent risk chapter that a test of details must be used as a response to significant risks. So if you have a complex estimate or fraud risk, develop a test of details, and link the identified significant risk to the planned audit steps.

Now let's see how you can best develop your procedures.

Selection of Procedures

Pay attention to the nature of each risk. Doing so allows you to determine the what, when, and degree of your procedures. The audit standards refer to this as the nature, timing, and extent. So, here is the way to design appropriate responses to your client's risks of material misstatement.

1. Nature of Evidence

First, consider the type of procedures, or the nature of evidence (as the audit standards call it). If an auditor believes that receivables might be overstated, then she might send confirmations to customers. Why confirmations? To prove the existence of the receivables.

Now compare the audit of receivables—which tends to be high risk—with that of prepaid assets—which is usually low risk. And why is it low risk? Prepaid assets is not complex. Prepaid assets is not an estimate and the volume of transactions is low. So, in this instance, the auditor could use substantive analytics— possibly a comparison of the account balance with prior years— which is more efficient than a test of details (e.g., recomputing the prepaid asset).

Risk drives the nature of the evidence needed (or the type of procedures to be used).

In addition to the nature of evidence, timing matters as well.

2. Timing of Evidence

So, should you perform audit procedures prior to the period-end? The answer depends on the reliability of the accounting system. Perform interim work when the accounting system is reliable, but consider waiting until period-end to audit unreliable systems. Why? If your interim work exposes significant accounting problems, you may not be comfortable with roll-forward procedures. In other words, you may have to re-perform your interim work after the period-end.

Do you perform a search for unrecorded liabilities? Then wait at least three or four weeks from period-end before you perform this procedure. The entity must receive invoices and make payments after period-end before you can review them. Likewise, if you are examining subsequent period receivable collections, allow a few weeks to pass before performing this procedure. For a December year-end, you might wait until mid-February before you test subsequent collections.

In addition to the nature and timing, the quantity of information is critical.

3. Extent of Evidence

The extent or quantity of evidence is another decision. Higher risks call for more evidence. If accounts payable has been materially understated the last two years, then consider lowering your search-for-unrecorded-liabilities threshold. If you've used $10,000, you could, for example, move it to $3,000. The lower threshold will yield more evidence. The main point here is you need more evidential matter as risk increases.

But can you audit too much information? The answer is yes—unless you have an unlimited time budget (and I bet you don't). Therefore, you want to examine enough information without overdoing it.

A question to ask in designing your quantity is *Will this test allow me to detect a material misstatement?* For instance, you might plan a sample. But once you total the individually significant items, you see the remaining amount is immaterial. If this is true, then you might test the individually significant items and stop.

Choosing Your Tests of Details

So there you have it: a summary of nature, timing, and extent. Learning to match your procedures with risks is one of the most important things you'll do as an auditor. Using canned audit programs or the same-as-last-year approach can lead to significant disconnects between your risk assessment and planned responses. Therefore, know your risks, and then design and perform responsive procedures.

Next we look at the second further audit procedure: substantive analytics.

Test of Details - A Simple Summary

- Test of details are required in all audits and include actions such as vouching invoices, testing bank reconciliations, and vouching subsequent receipts
- A test of details is required for significant risks
- The nature, timing, and extent of further audit procedures should be in response to the risks of material misstatement

CHAPTER 20
Substantive Analytics

Are you using substantive analytics in your audits? Many auditors rely solely on tests of details when a better option is available. Substantive analytics, in some cases, provide better evidential matter, and they are often more efficient than tests of details.

Professional standards define analytical procedures as evaluations of financial and non-financial data with plausible relationships. In other words, numbers behave in particular ways, and because they do, we can evaluate these relationships and use them as a risk assessment tool and as evidential matter for our audit opinions.

This chapter focuses on substantive analytics. But before we look at what substantive analytics are and how to use them, let's see how analytical procedures are used in audits.

Analytics in Three Stages

Auditors use analytics in three stages:

1. Preliminary (risk assessment)
2. Final (wrap up)
3. Substantive (response to risks of material misstatement)

Preliminary analytics are performed as a risk assessment procedure. (See the Preliminary Analytical Procedures chapter.) We use them to locate potential material misstatements. And if we identify unexpected activity, we plan a response. For example, if we expect payroll to go up 5% but it goes down 8%, then we plan further audit procedures to see why.

At the completion of the audit, we use final analytics to determine if we have addressed all risks of material misstatement. Here we compare our numbers and ask, *Have we dealt with all risks of material misstatement?* If yes, fine. If not, then we may need to perform additional audit procedures.

Less precision is necessary for preliminary and final analytics as compared to substantive analytics. Preliminary analytics are used to locate potential misstatements, and final analytics are used to confirm the results of the audit. But substantive analytics are used to prove material misstatements are not present, and, as such, provide evidential matter for the auditor's opinion.

Substantive Analytics

Substantive analytics can, in certain cases, be more effective and efficient than a test of details.

For example, if the ratio of salaries to total expenses has been in the 46% to 48% range for the last few years, then you can use this ratio as a substantive analytic to prove the payroll occurrence assertion. If your expectation is that payroll would be in this range and your computation yields 48%, then your substantive analytic provides evidence that the salaries occurred. And this is much easier than a test of details such as a test of forty payroll transactions (where you might agree hours paid to time records and payroll rates to authorized amounts).

Disaggregation

For a small entity with six employees, one payroll substantive analytic might be sufficient, but you may need to disaggregate payroll for a larger company with six hundred people. For example, you might divide departmental salaries by total salaries and compare those ratios to the prior year. Disaggregation adds more precision to the analytic, resulting in better evidential matter.

Another example of disaggregation is in relation to revenues. If the company has four major sources of revenue, disaggregate the substantive analytical revenue sources. You might use a trend analysis by revenue source for the last three years. Or you might recompute an estimate of one or more revenue sources based on units sold or property rented.

The type of substantive analytic is dependent on the nature of the transaction or account balance. If a company rents fifty apartments at the same monthly rate, computing an estimate of revenue is easy. But if a company sells fifty different products at different prices, you may need to disaggregate the substantive analytical data.

Additionally, consider disaggregating substantive analytics by region if the company has different geographic locations.

Significant Risk Response

Are there audit areas where substantive analytics should not be used alone? Yes, there is an area: when responding to a significant risk. A test of details must be used when a significant risk is present. For example, a bank's allowance for loan losses is a significant risk. This allowance is a highly complex estimate; therefore, a test of details is required. You could not solely compare the allowance to prior years, for example, though such a comparison could complement a test of details. In other words, you could perform a test of details *and* use a substantive analytic, but a substantive analytic alone would not do.

Now let's consider how auditors use substantive analytics to respond to risks of material misstatement.

Responses to Risks of Material Misstatement

Once we identify risks of material misstatement, we plan further audit procedures. Many auditors use a test of details without performing substantive analytics. Why? For many, it's habit. For example, you might have always vouched sixty disbursements to invoices on a sample basis (to verify expenses), so you continue to do so; but maybe you've never used substantive analytics to prove expenses.

Substantive Analytics for Predictable Areas

Substantive analytics are often more fitting for income statement accounts such as revenue or expenses. Why? Because income statement account balances tend to be consistent from year to year. Here are some examples:

- Depreciation expense
- Payroll expense
- Lease revenue
- Property tax revenue (in a government)

So consider using substantive analytics when the volume of transactions is high and the account balance is predictable.

Substantive Analytics for Lower Risk Areas

Additionally, use substantive analytics in lower risk areas, including some balance sheet accounts such as:

- Plant, property, and equipment (when there are no significant additions or retirements)
- Debt (when there is little debt activity)
- Prepaid assets (when activity is similar year-to-year)

Audit standards tell us that substantive analytics are more appropriate when the risk of misstatement is lower. The higher the risk of misstatement, the more you should use a test of details. For instance, it's better to use tests of details for significant receivable accounts, but substantive analytics may work well for prepaid insurance.

Combined Audit Approach

Additionally, substantive analytics can be combined with a test of details or a test of controls. If, for example, you're planning a risk response for accounts payable and expenses, you might use a combined approach: a test of details for accounts payable (e.g., search for unrecorded liabilities) and substantive analytics for expense (e.g., departmental expenses divided by total expenses compared to the prior year).

Another common combined approach is a test of details sample along with substantive analytics. If the substantive analytics are effective, you can reduce the test of details sample size, making the overall approach more efficient.

Substantive Analytical Procedures Assurance Level

Certain substantive analytics provide higher levels of assurance. For example, computing expected rental income provides high assurance. If your client rents fifty identical apartments at $2,000 a month, the computation is easy and the assurance is high.

But other types of analytics provide less assurance: for example, topside ratios or period-to-period comparisons at the financial statement level. However, you can increase the substantive analytical assurance level by taking actions such as:

- Using more comparative periods (e.g., years or months)
- Comparing ratios to independently published industry statistics
- Disaggregating the data (e.g., revenues by product line and units sold)

- Documenting expectations prior to creating the analytics (to remove bias)
- Documenting client responses regarding unexpected differences along with your follow up procedures and results

Comparing balances with a prior period and providing no explanations is not sufficient as a substantive analytic. Also, if changes in balances are unexpected, inquiring of the client about those changes and documenting vague client responses is not sufficient. For example, these client answers will not do:

- *Client expected revenues to go up*
- *Numbers declined because sales activity went down*
- *Client said it's reasonable*

Vague responses are not evidential matter and can result in audit failure, or—worse yet—litigation against your firm. Such responses will also draw fire from your peer reviewer.

Substantive analytics, when created appropriately, can be used in a wide variety of ways.

Examples of Substantive Analytics

Here are examples of substantive analytics:

- Comparison of monthly sales for the current year with that of the preceding year (to test occurrence)
- Comparison of profit margins for the last few months of the audit period with those subsequent to period-end (to test cutoff)
- Comparison of the percent of expenses to sales with the prior year (to test occurrence)
- Current ratio compared to prior year (to test for solvency and going concern)
- Comparing current year profit margins with prior periods (to test accuracy and occurrence)

- For pension or post-employment benefit plans: actuarial value of plan assets divided by actuarial accrued liability compared to prior year (to test completeness and accuracy)
- For debt: total debt divided by total assets compared to prior year (to test the financial strength of the entity and going concern)
- For inventory: cost of goods sold divided by average inventory compared to prior year (to test existence and occurrence)
- For expenses: comparison of recorded amounts with budgeted expenses (to test occurrence)

Now let's see how to document substantive analytics.

Documentation of Substantive Analytics

In performing substantive analytics, document the following:

1. **The reliability of the data**

    Document why you believe the data is trustworthy. Reasons could include your prior experience with the client's accounting system and internal controls related to the information you are using. Though a walkthrough sheds light on those controls, a test of controls for effectiveness provides even greater support for the reliability of the data. Testing controls is optional, but audit standards intimate a preference for such tests in proving the reliability of data. For example, if you compute sales revenue based on units sold, you might test the controls related to this non-financial information. You might also test the operating effectiveness of controls related to sales revenue, the financial information.

2. **Assessed risks of material misstatement by assertion**

    Document the assertions being addressed and the related risks of material misstatement.

3. **Expectation**

    Document a sufficiently precise expected result of the computation or comparison. You can use a range. Document the expectation prior to examining the recorded numbers. Why? To reduce bias. If the current year expectation is different from the prior year, explain why. For example, if payroll has been stable over the last three years but is expected to increase eight percent in the current year, document why. A less precise expectation may be acceptable if a test of details is performed along with the substantive analytic.

4. **Approach**

    Document if the substantive analytic is to be used alone or in conjunction with a test of details or a test of controls.

5. **Acceptable difference**

    The acceptable difference is the amount that requires no further investigation. So, for example, if the analytic is $30,000 different from the recorded amount and the acceptable difference is $50,000, you are done. No additional work is necessary. Unacceptable differences require further investigation such as inquiries of management and other audit procedures. Consider the performance materiality for the transaction or account balance as you develop the acceptable difference amount. Also, consider the assessed risk of material misstatement. As risk increases, lower the acceptable difference.

6. **Conclusion**

    Document whether the computation or comparison falls within your expectation. Perform and document other procedures performed if the result is not within your acceptable difference. Your conclusion should include a statement regarding whether you believe the account or transaction balance is materially correct. After all, that's the purpose of the substantive analytic.

Here are some concluding thoughts about substantive analytics.

Substantive Analytical Considerations

Substantive analytics are not required, so think of them as an efficient alternative to test of details.

If the company has weak internal controls or a history of significant misstatements, rely more on tests of details. Substantive analytics work better in stable environments. Additionally, if you, as the auditor, expect to make several material audit adjustments, record those prior to creating substantive analytics. For example, make sure all payables are recorded. This will reduce the distortion from those misstatements.

Testing of controls for effectiveness lends strength to substantive analytics. If the controls are effective, you'll have more confidence in the substantive analytics. For example, if you test the disbursement approval controls and find them to be effective, the expense analytics will be more trustworthy. If you are testing controls for effectiveness, you may want to do so before creating any related substantive analytics.

The most common substantive analytical deficiencies are:

- Comparing current and prior year numbers and documenting vague client explanations regarding differences
- No documented expectations

Next, we will look at the third further audit procedure: test of controls.

Substantive Analytics - A Simple Summary

- Analytical procedures are evaluations of financial and non-financial data with plausible relationships
- Substantive analytics are evidential matter supporting an audit opinion and are a response to risks of material

misstatement; preliminary analytics are used to identify risks of material misstatement
- Substantive analytics are enhanced by:
  - Disaggregating data
  - Using more comparative periods
  - Developing and documenting expectations prior to creating the analytics
  - Comparing ratios to independently published industry statistics
  - Documenting client responses along with follow up procedures
  - Performing a test of controls related to the substantive analytical data
- Substantive analytics are useful for predictable transaction cycles such as payroll
- Substantive analytics are suitable for lower risk areas; a test of details is more suitable for higher risk areas
- Document substantive analytical information such as:
  - Reliability of the data
  - Assessed risks of material misstatement by assertion
  - Expectations
  - Approach (substantive analytics alone or in combination with a test of details or a test of controls)
  - Acceptable difference
  - Conclusion

CHAPTER 21
Test of Controls

Which responses to risks of material misstatement are best: substantive procedures or a test of controls? That depends on what you discover in risk assessment.

If, for example, your client consistently fails to record payables, then assess control risk for completeness at high and perform a search for unrecorded liabilities (a substantive procedure).

By contrast, if the internal controls for receivables are strong, then assess control risk for the existence assertion at less than high, and test controls for effectiveness. You do, however, have the option to perform substantive tests rather than test controls, even when controls are working appropriately.

Not Testing Controls

As we said in the Control Risk chapter, many auditors assess control risk at high (after risk assessment is complete) and use a fully substantive approach. That is fine, especially in audits of smaller entities. Why? Because smaller entities tend to have weak controls. As a result, controls may not be effective. Therefore, you may not be able to assess control risk at less than high.

Control risk assessments of less than high must be supported with a test of controls proving their effectiveness. But if controls are not effective, control risk must be assessed at high. This is one reason why you might bypass testing controls: you know, either from prior experience or from current-year walkthroughs, that controls are not effective.

The Decision about Testing Controls

But if controls are effective, why not test them? Doing so allows you to reduce your substantive procedures. There is one reason, however, why you might not test controls even though they appear appropriate: substantive procedures may take less time than tests of controls (as we saw in the Control Risk chapter).

Once risk assessment is complete, your responses (the further audit procedures) are based on efficiency and effectiveness. If control testing takes less time, then test controls. If substantive procedures takes less time, then perform a test of details or use substantive analytics. But, regardless of efficiency considerations, address all risks with appropriate responses.

So, are you ever required to test controls?

Required Test of Controls

There are two situations where you must test controls:

- When there is a significant risk and you are placing reliance on controls related to that risk
- When substantive procedures don't properly address a risk of material misstatement

Auditing standards allow a three-year rotation for control testing, as long as the area tested is not a significant risk. But if the auditor plans to rely on a test of controls related to a significant risk, operating effectiveness must be tested annually. (I explain the three-year rotation option below.)

Also, a test of controls is necessary if substantive procedures don't properly address a risk of material misstatement. Some highly automated transactions may be difficult to address with substantive procedures. If you find that substantive procedures will not properly address the risks of material misstatement, then a test of controls may be your only choice. In most cases, substantive procedures can be used, so the requirement to test controls is usually not relevant.

Now you know about required control tests. But what about optional control testing?

Optional Test of Controls

You must test controls for the two situations just described, if they are present. All other control testing is optional, but prior to making the decision to test controls, consider the following:

- Do you anticipate effectiveness? There's no need to test an ineffective control.
- Does the control relate to an assertion for which you desire a lower control risk?
- Will it take less time to test the control than to perform a substantive procedure? Sometimes you may not know the answer to this question until you perform the test of controls. If the initial test does not prove effectiveness, then you have to expand your sample size or just punt; in other words, use a fully substantive approach.
- Will you use the test of controls in conjunction with a test of details or substantive analytics? How would effective controls reduce these substantive tests? In other words, how much substantive testing time can you save if the control is effective?
- Is the control evidence physical or electronic? For example, are the entity's receipts in a physical receipt book or in a computer? It's usually easier to test electronic evidence.
- How large will your sample size be? Some controls occur once a month. Others, thousands of times in the period. The larger the population, the larger the sample. And, of course, the larger the sample size, the more time it will take to test the control.

- Can you test the population as a whole without sampling? In some instances data analytics software can be used to test the entire population. For example, if a purchase order is required for all payments above $5,000, it might be easy to compare all payments above the threshold to purchase orders, assuming the purchase orders are electronic.

Three-Year Rotation of Control Testing

As I said earlier, audit standards allow a three-year rotation for control testing. For example, if you test accounts payable controls in 20X0, then you can wait until 20X3 to test them again. In 20X1 and 20X2, you need to ensure that these controls have not changed. You also want to determine that those controls have continuing relevance in the current audit. How? See if the controls continue to address a risk of material misstatement. And as you perform your annual walkthroughs, inquire about changes, observe the controls, and inspect documents. Why? You want to know that everything is working as it was in 20X0, when the initial test was performed. And, yes, you do need to perform those walkthroughs *annually* (if that is how you corroborate your understanding of controls).

In short, testing of controls for effectiveness can, in most cases, occur every three years. But walkthroughs are necessary each year. If you tested sixty transactions—using a sample—for appropriate purchase orders in 20X0, then you can wait until 20X3 to do so again. However, be sure to review the purchase order process each year in your annual walkthroughs.

So should you test controls at interim or after year-end?

Interim or Period-End Control Tests

Some auditors test controls after the period-end (after year-end in most cases); others at interim. Which is best?

It depends.

Perform interim test of controls if this fits better in your work schedule. Here's an example: You perform an interim test of controls on November 1, 20X1. Later, say in February 20X2, consider whether controls have changed during the last two months of the year. See if the same people are performing those controls. Furthermore, consider performing additional tests of controls for the November 1 to December 31 period. Once done, determine if the controls are effective.

Testing on an interim date is not always the answer. For example, if management is inclined to manipulate earnings near year-end, then interim tests may not be appropriate.

If you choose to test controls after period-end, then do so for the full period being audited. For instance, test the period January 1 through December 31 for a calendar year business. Your sample should be representative of that timeframe.

Point-in-Time Controls

So should you ever test controls at a point in time and not over a period of time? Yes, sometimes. For example, test inventory count controls at year-end only (if counts are done once a year). Why? Well those controls are only relevant to the year-end count, a point in time. Most controls, however, are in use throughout the period you are auditing. Therefore, you need to test those controls over that period of time (e.g., year).

Well we're almost done. Just one more chapter, in which we'll review three common audit planning mistakes. I bet you've seen one or more of these.

Test of Controls - A Simple Summary

- Test of controls is a further audit procedure used to gain evidential matter to support an audit opinion
- A test of controls is required in two instances:
  - When there is a significant risk and the auditor is placing reliance on controls related to that risk
  - When substantive procedures don't properly address a risk of material misstatement
- When transaction cycle walkthroughs (a risk assessment procedure) reveal that controls are appropriately designed and implemented, the auditor has two options:
  - Assess control risk at high and not test controls for effectiveness
  - Assess control risk below high and test controls for effectiveness
- When control risk is assessed below high, a test of controls must be performed and the test must show that the controls are effective; the test of controls is the basis for the lower risk assessment
- Controls can be tested every third year provided the control is not related to a significant risk; even so, walkthroughs should be performed annually to ensure the control is still appropriately designed and implemented
- Controls can be tested at an interim date provided management is not inclined to manipulate earnings

CHAPTER 22
Three Audit Planning Mistakes

Auditors make three common planning mistakes: (1) not tailoring audit programs, (2) allowing prior year work papers to drive the audit process, and (3) using a balance sheet audit approach. Let's see how these happen.

1. Not Tailoring Audit Programs

Where do most audit programs come from? They are purchased from forms providers, usually international publishing companies. These purchased programs are useful, but they can become a crutch, leading to canned audit approaches that are not responsive to risks.

If we use unrevised audit programs and if our audit approach is always the same, what good is risk assessment? Another way to say this is, *If audit programs never change, why perform walkthroughs, preliminary analytics, and other risk assessment procedures?*

Canned audit programs are one reason auditors give lip-service to risk assessment. The auditor may be thinking, *I already know what I'm going to do, so why waste time with risk assessment?* This cookie-cutter approach is dangerous, but quite common. And why is it dangerous? Because it can lead to an intentional blindness toward internal controls and significant risks. And deficiencies in risk assessment can lead to deficiencies in audit procedures. The potential result: material misstatements are not identified and an incorrect audit opinion is issued. In other words, audit failure occurs.

Audit programs can be tailored: steps can be added, changed, or deleted based on the risks of material misstatement. But some auditors don't change their audit plan, and not tailoring audit programs can lead to several problems such as:

- Audit team members signing off on steps not performed
- Team members typing *Not Applicable* (N/A) next to several audit steps
- Auditors performing unnecessary procedures
- Auditors not performing needed procedures

In addition to not tailoring audit programs, some auditors hit autopilot and use their prior year work papers as their current year plan.

2. Prior Year Work Papers as the Audit Plan

Audit documentation should generally develop in the following manner:

1. Risk assessment
2. Audit programs
3. Further audit procedures

But poor auditors tend to follow the prior year work papers and complete the audit program as an afterthought. Worse yet, the risk assessment work is completed at the end of the engagement, if at all. The tail wags the dog. This same-as-last-year approach leads to incongruities in risks of material misstatement and the procedures performed. In effect, the prior year work papers become the current year audit program.

Another common audit planning mistake is the use of a balance sheet audit approach.

3. Balance Sheet Audit Approach

As we saw in the Control Risk chapter, many auditors use a fully substantive approach, meaning they don't test controls for effectiveness. Moreover, some auditors test balance sheet accounts and little else. But this approach can lead to problems.

I have heard auditors say: *If I audit all of the balance sheet accounts, then the only thing that can be wrong is the composition of revenues and expenses.* But is this true?

The accounting equation says:

Totals assets = Total liabilities plus Total equity

Another way to say this is:

Total equity = Total assets minus Total liabilities

If we disregard stock purchases and sales, equity is usually the accumulation of retained earnings. And retained earnings comes from the earnings or losses on the income statement. In other words, retained earnings comes from revenues and expenses. So the net income or loss (revenues minus expenses) has to fit into the accounting equation (equity equals assets minus liabilities).

Therefore, if we audit all assets and liability accounts, doesn't it make sense *that the only thing that can be wrong is the composition of revenues and expenses?* Mathematically I see why someone might say this, but a flaw lurks in this construct.

I once watched a company sue an audit firm for several million dollars. The CPA firm had audited the company for many years and issued an unqualified opinion each year, but a material theft was occurring all along.

And what was the nature of the fraud? A key accounting person controlled the payroll process (with no segregation of duties), and he exploited this internal control weakness by wiring fraudulent payments to his personal bank account. As he did, the salary expense increased dramatically, but the auditors ignored the obvious.

So what were the audit firm's mistakes? They relied too much on a balance sheet audit approach, and they did not gain an understanding of the company's key internal controls.

The auditors used substantive procedures such as:

- Testing bank reconciliations
- Sending receivable confirmations and vouching subsequent collections
- Computing annual depreciation and agreeing it to the general ledger
- Vouching additions to plant, property, and equipment
- Performing a search for unrecorded liabilities in payables
- Confirming debt

The balance sheet accounts reconciled to the general ledger, and no problems were noted in the audit of the balance sheet accounts. But millions were missing, and payroll expense was overstated.

So what flaw lies in a balance sheet audit approach? Millions can go missing while the balance sheet accounts reconcile to the general ledger. Consequently, auditing the balance sheet accounts alone may not detect theft. Therefore, gaining an understanding of the internal controls and developing appropriate responses is critical to identifying material misstatements, especially when fraud is possible. And it always is.

So as we plan our audit procedures, we need to avoid the flawed balance sheet approach. Yes, substantive procedures for the balance sheet accounts are important, but fraud detection procedures are necessary when control weaknesses are present.

Three Audit Planning Mistakes - A Simple Summary

- Three common audit planning mistakes include:
  - Not tailoring audit programs in response to risks of material misstatement
  - Allowing prior year work papers to drive the current year audit process without consideration for current year risks of material misstatement
  - Using a balance sheet audit approach and ignoring internal controls and the potential for fraud

CONCLUSION

Let the wise hear and increase in learning.
- Proverbs 1:5

Now you understand audit risk assessment.

It starts with client acceptance and continues all the way through the conclusion of your audit.

Early in the engagement, you perform risk assessment procedures such as walkthroughs, fraud inquiries, preliminary analytics, retrospective reviews of estimates, and gaining an understanding of the entity and its environment. And as risks of material misstatement are identified, you place them on the auditor's risk assessment summary form.

Once those risks are summarized, you use them to assess inherent risks and control risks. And these inform your decisions regarding risks of material misstatement at the assertion level for accounts, transaction cycles, and disclosures. Inherent risk, control risk, and the risk of material misstatement are normally assessed at low, moderate, or high, though other levels of measurement can be used.

The risk assessment summary includes risks at the financial statement level and at the assertion level in accounts balances, transaction classes, and disclosures.

Financial statement level risks are pervasive in nature and require general responses such as the use of more experienced staff.

Assertion level risks are specific to account balances, transaction cycles, and disclosures. Those risks are addressed with further audit procedures, including tests of details, substantive analytics, and test of controls for effectiveness. Moreover, these procedures are specified in audit programs for areas such as cash, receivables, and debt.

Additionally, an audit strategy is created. It specifies information such as planned completion dates, audit staff, overall objectives, and the scope of the engagement.

If you encounter additional risks as you perform the planned audit procedures, reconsider your initial risk assessments and planning information, and amend those, if necessary.

As you've seen throughout this book, risk assessment is foundational to all successful audits. My hope is that with this information you will perform future engagements with rising confidence, and that you'll find audit risk assessment useful—and maybe, just maybe, even enjoyable.

AUTHOR INFORMATION

Charles Hall is a Certified Public Accountant in the United States. He frequently speaks at continuing education events for CPAs and is a blogger at CPAHallTalk.com.

This is Charles' fourth book, the first being *The Little Book of Local Government Fraud Prevention*, the second, *Preparation of Financial Statements and Compilation Engagements*, the third, *The Why and How of Auditing*.

Charles is the quality control partner at McNair, McLemore, Middlebrooks & Co, LLC in Macon, Georgia. As such, he works with audit professionals on a daily basis. Charles also consults with CPA firms throughout the United States. He has audited governments, nonprofits, and commercial entities since 1985.

Charles received his Master's Degree in Accounting from the University of Georgia in 1984.

Made in United States
North Haven, CT
20 August 2024